A Double Bassist's Guide to Refining Performance Practices

A Double Bassist's Guide to Refining Performance Practices

Murray Grodner

Indiana University Press
Bloomington and Indianapolis

This book is a publication of

Indiana University Press
Office of Scholarly Publishing
Herman B Wells Library 350
1320 East Tenth Street
Bloomington, Indiana 47405 USA

iupress.indiana.edu

Telephone orders   800-842-6796
Fax orders   812-855-7931

© 2013 by Murray Grodner

All rights reserved

No part of this book may be reproduced or utilized in any form or by any means, electronic or mechanical, including photocopying and recording, or by any information storage and retrieval system, without permission in writing from the publisher. The Association of American University Presses' Resolution on Permissions constitutes the only exception to this prohibition.

∞ The paper used in this publication meets the minimum requirements of the American National Standard for Information Sciences--Permanence of Paper for Printed Library Materials, ANSI Z39.48-1992.

Manufactured in the United States of America

Cataloging information is available from the Library of Congress.

ISBN 978-0-253-01016-2 (pbk)
ISBN 978-0-253-01020-9 (eb)

        1 2 3 4 5 18 17 16 15 14 13

Contents

Preface	vii
Part I. Critical Analysis of Physical Performance Techniques	**1**
Use of Self	1
Toward Creating a More Competent Bassist	2
Practice Habits	3
The Left Arm and Hand	4
The Shifting Process	6
Ah Yes, Vibrato	7
The Bow Arm	10
Sound Production	14
More Thoughts on Performance Practices	16
How Much Input of Energy is Too Much?	17
Developing an Automatically Responsive Bow Arm and Left Hand/Arm	18
How to Problem Solve	20
Perfecting and Resolving Techniques	22
Scales	22
Part II. Perfecting Techniques through Employing Scales, Exercises, and Orchestral Excerpts	**25**
1. Essential Bowings to Use in Scales	26
2- and 3-Octave Scales (3 sets of fingerings)	51
2- and 3-Octave Arpeggio Fingerings	61
Chromatic Scales	63
String Crossing Exercises	70
Trill, Finger, and Shifting Exercises	72
2. Related Orchestral Excerpts	77
Part III. Informative Essays for Double Bassists	**101**
"Basses, You Are Late."	101
Chamber Music	102
French Bow vs. German Bow	102
Auditions and Recitals	104
Thoughts Concerning Teaching	105
Thoughts Concerning Directions for a Professional Career	106
Musical Education for Public School Music Teaching	107
Orchestral Training	109
Music Schools and Education of Orchestral Musicians	110
Summers	111
Some Recommendations for Setting Up and Buying a Double Bass	112
Awareness and Knowledge Necessary When Considering the Purchase of a Double Bass	115
Information for Purchasing a Fine Bow	116

Contents

Part IV. Analytical Phrasing and Bowing for Solo Works — 119

    Legato Phrasing: The Age of *Portamento* vs. the Slur — 119
    Interpretation and Phrasing — 119
    Prelude from Second Suite for Cello by J.S. Bach — 121
    Dragonetti and Koussevitzky Concertos — 124

Part V. Preventative Exercises for Physical Abuses Related to Playing Double Bass — 143

    It's Usually Too Late When We Say, "I Wish I Had!" — 143
    "Playing Positions and Related Biochemical Issues,"
        by Chris Gales, Physical Therapist — 145

Preface

Titling this book has been a challenge. Although it may seem geared to the advanced student (like those) studying at schools like Julliard and the Jacobs School of Music, it also contains areas pertinent to the interest of the advanced professional bassist. Some of the subject matter may seem basic, but it really consists of challenges that may not have been conquered by performers at all levels. I have never stopped warming up with the scales, bowings, and exercises in Section IIA of this book. Each session was devoted to improving control, articulation, and facility for each example included that day.

My intent is to make each reader think more about "use of self"; to make one aware of the techniques we are required to use and cause us to re-examine them based on an analytical awareness that will be provided. Comprehension and analysis bring results that time and effort alone may not provide. My hope is that this work will encourage a re-evaluation and further understanding of use of self while making one's ultimate efforts to perform on the double bass.

I am indebted to Michael Sweeney, who created the notation and patiently endured the many changes and reformatting required. His computer prowess allowed for the physical creation of the final product.

My love and gratitude to my wife, Susan, who made my work on this opus possible by the constant patience she displayed with my being closeted for hours and days during this effort. She was subjected to listening and reacting to thoughts that evolved during the creating of this book. Her patience and interest inspired me to keep going until the effort was complete. In truth, however, books like this seem never to be finished. There is always more to explore and discuss, but I hope the work opens doors for continued thought about why we perform as we do and a more efficient "use of self."

A Double Bassist's Guide to Refining Performance Practices

PART 1

Critical Analysis of Physical Performance Techniques

Use of Self

In reading this book you will find the phrase "use of self" employed a number of times. I was asked by a reader of the original manuscript to clarify the meaning and reason for use of this phrase.

You may be familiar with the Alexander Technique. I took several lessons from various teachers of this philosophy of physical behavior. Initially, the Alexander teacher "maneuvered" head, neck and shoulders, and said little, leaving me wondering what I was supposed to take with me from the lesson. For a long time I was never quite sure what I was supposed to learn from the experience. Sometime later I found an Alexander teacher who was more verbal. I brought a bass to one lesson and we explored physical challenges presented by the double bass, experimenting with various positions suggested by the Alexander teacher. It became obvious that there really is not a perfect solution for physically dealing with the size of our instrument. There is only the most appropriate physical adaptation to an instrument the size and shape of the double bass. As time went by, I believe I found the answer to the goal of the Alexander teacher and my investigation of the possibility of physical positioning for playing double bass. It is the same goal that teachers of double bass should constantly be working toward: *making the best use of self*. Although I am not positive, I believe this might also be one of the goals of the Alexander system. If not, unquestionably the premise to make "best use of self" is. This goal is essential for the most successful fulfillment of our physical and musical aspirations.

The question now becomes, what is the best use of self? Who determines that? We play a large instrument that challenges us to find the most comfortable manner in which to maneuver on it and extract meaningful sounds. Our teachers' intent is to help us achieve these goals, but there is still the question, is our success really being achieved through best "use of self"? Are all teachers successful in teaching and making best "use of self"? Are we as teachers passing on what we have learned from experience by exploring how to translate our knowledge, or are we primarily leaning on what we learned from our teachers, without further questioning or enlarging on that information? Making best "use of self" requires translating musical thoughts and efforts through positive physical and intellectual application. Such is the goal of this book.

As you will find when reading on, I attempt to analyze and organize all aspects involved with positive performance, providing reasoning for the solutions suggested to hopefully make best "use of self."

The last chapter, written by Chris Gale, a physical therapist, results from awareness that proper "use of self" alone does not prevent physical abuse resulting from years of using the physical self to play double bass. We are not alone in experiencing this problem. The violinist and violist are even more subject to abusive behavior resulting from their required playing posture. The flutist is physically unbalanced by having to constantly hold his or her arms up shifted to the right. Even the clarinetist suffers from discomfort of the thumb that is placed below the metal thumb support. The only performers that seem to be less physically abused are the percussionists. Their abuse, however, can be damage to their hearing that results from the volume and percussive "explosions" required for performing on that family of instruments.

Although there may not be a perfect physical means of performing on our instrument, it is possible and essential for us to make best "use of self" physically, technically, musically, and intellectually.

Toward Creating a More Competent Bassist

(A guide for identifying, analyzing and resolving musical performance challenges, including treatises on the various aspects of the ever-evolving musician.)

It is interesting to note that, besides professional musicians, many doctors and individuals in some of the other sciences play an orchestral instrument. There are doctors' orchestras in several American cities. I had quite talented students who were practicing physicians, and I have performed chamber music with groups made up of only doctors. They were musically very competent and dedicated, providing me with a musical experience in many ways equal to performing with similar ensembles of fine professional musicians.

It is believed that the part(s) of the brain used by musicians and certain members of the sciences are closely related. A good doctor has to be very analytical and innovative in order to deal with the variety of symptoms and types of individuals that confront him or her for their medical needs. No one dies if a musician errs in performance, but it would enhance our abilities to perform and teach if we were as analytical in our musical creativity and solution of performance problems as are competent physicians in diagnoses based on physical symptoms.

This book is an effort to encourage one to make more conscious use of the part of the brain we seem to share with those in the sciences, resulting in more analytical problem solving for musical performance.

Tendencies of both teachers and players are to associate playing with the hands rather than the totality of integrated behavior between the mind, body, legs, arms, and hands. Have you considered that left hand is an initiator of motion (only) when fingering in a single position, while the right hand is never an initiator?

Staying aware of bowing will make you realize that the arm moves the hand before the hand ever flexes, and the hand primarily responds to the arm's motions. The fingers of the right hand respond to the tug on the hand (that is being moved by the arm) and to the resistance met by the bow being pressed against and pulled across the string. In this process, weight/pressure and direction are provided by the arm.

Even before all of these movements occur, there should be an automatic preparation of balancing the body, anticipating the leverage required to move the bow arm with proper energy for producing sound and rhythms. There also needs to be an anticipation of the role and response of the hand to the motion of the arm and the rhythmic requirements of musical notation.

All of this occurs more automatically or instinctively through practice and training, if one is properly instructed for necessary comprehension to evolve. It doesn't seem very complicated, does it? Then why do so many string players play as if all great technical feats result from primarily focusing on hands and fingers? Without the arms, the hands can go nowhere. We shift with the arm. We vibrate with the arm. We bow primarily with our arms. Unnecessary tension results from improper focus on what is mechanically responsible for the various aspects of our physical performance. Perceiving the hands as responsible for what only the arms can (should) do creates improper focus. This results in frustrations for finding solutions to performance problems and creates mental and physical tensions.

A large portion of this book will deal with proper balancing, shaping and motion, as well as assigning specific responsibility to the main body parts used in the various aspects of physical performance. Too much muscular tension and disoriented mental concepts exist; that can be helped by analytical observations, recommended corrections, and other musical suggestions included in this treatise. Start this journey by thinking of the above references to the mechanics of a properly initiated bow stroke.

Practice Habits

Using practice time most fruitfully means organization of the practice period plus being aurally very aware and intellectually analytical.

Time and again I have heard "I have practiced this passage at least one hundred times and when I come back to it again, I may still make the same mistakes. Why?" Note the part of this statement that says "the same mistakes." It should be obvious that there is a problem in the passage that remains unsolved, or one would not continue to have a result that causes the "same mistakes." Learning by repetition will work for passages that contain technical problems that have already been resolved by the player, consciously or instinctively. However, not being able to master a passage will be due to either the limitations of a player's level of performance or one's lack of having learned or recognized the technique that could avoid the stumbling. The problem is likely one of the many left-hand or bowing techniques not yet not learned or mastered. Basically, you can't play the first movement of Beethoven's Symphony no. 7, if you haven't learned to master the recurring bowing:

One may not successfully play the arpeggiated passages in Heldenleben without recognizing the tendency of the left hand to rush the first triplet of the arpeggio and/or the B-flat sixteenth before resolution note E-flat. These notes are not firmly executed by both bow and fingers because we are so anxious about getting to where we are going. We actually don't allow enough time to properly articulate bow and left hand so that these notes can be clearly heard. The problem in the Beethoven, as I already mentioned, is not having resolved the bowing problem, while in Heldenleben it is lack of clarity due to not knowing how to take the time to allow the arpeggios to sound clearly. Unaware repetitive practicing of these problem passages may make them sound better, but not recognizing or resolving their inherent problems will more likely end in a result that is not fully controlled or aurally satisfying.

Proper use of practice time means learning how to control playing through analyzing problems and identifying the techniques that need correction. Isolate the technical problem(s) and create a brief exercise that allows analytical practicing to correct the technical flaw in your execution of this type of passage. This approach means using materials to develop the left hand and bow arm. It requires building a vocabulary of behavior that includes as many learned techniques as one can resolve, before encountering these challenges in a solo or orchestra work. Learning how to identify and solve technical difficulties will be discussed in depth, starting with the following section and continuing through the multiple pages that follow.

The Left Arm and Hand

POSITION (CONFIGURATION), FINGERING, SHIFTING, THUMB, VIBRATO

The left-hand thumb: Why should it be very modestly curved and not "straight"?

Place your left hand on the neck of the bass in your usual playing position. Press down normally on string and back of neck. Now straighten (unbend) the thumb's first joint as far as it can go, to the point at which it locks. Note (feel) the tension at the first joint of the thumb and the area of the web, between your thumb and 1st finger. Now very, very *modestly* allow the first joint of the thumb to unlock and curve (bend) slightly. Notice the difference in tension in the thumb joint and web area. The flat area (pad of thumb) should still be retaining contact with back of the neck of bass. It should not be placed so that only the very tip of thumb is in contact with neck. If one plays on tip of thumb rather than the flat (pad) of the thumb, other fingers will be somewhat pulled away from the strings. Placing the tip of thumb (relatively pointing) on the back of the neck decreases the access of the other fingers to the area of the strings and can be a source of unnecessary tension. Experiment with these positions of the thumb, noting the effect on tension and comfort. Remain very conscious of the effect the position and shape of the thumb have on access to the string and comfort of the 1st through 4th fingers. Done properly, the above recommendations should relax unnecessary tension and provide maximum access to the playing area of string.

Another important practice is allowing the thumb to move (rotate sparingly) across the back of the neck, when moving from string to string. This is especially necessary when moving to a string other than the immediately adjoining string. Finding a balance place on the neck for playing on adjoining strings is easily done. Adjusting the thumb for hand rotation to a string farther away helps retain the strongest and most maneuverable position for the hand/fingers. This also diminishes tension caused by unnecessarily reaching over to other than adjoining string. Any change to recommended physical practices will become habit over time through constant awareness and physical reinforcement.

At this point, it needs to be stated that there are at least two major kinds of tension. One is the type caused by the normal tendon and muscular support needed to hold us upright, to walk. or to do most other physical activities. Without the automatic muscular (supportive) tension required for daily activity, we would collapse into a sack of flesh and bones. Our concern, however, is only with excess or unnecessary tension caused by improper usage of body parts, or mental perceptions that cause improper usage. There is supportive tension in everything we do, including playing a musical instrument, but we must not make performing more difficult by creating situations that cause unneeded or excess tension.

Much has been said about left-hand thumb support for fingers and where the thumb should be placed in relation to the other fingers. There are, however, too many varied hand shapes (structures and sizes) for one formula to work for all hands. Some hands will not comfortably or properly allow the thumb to be placed opposite the 2nd finger, as is so often prescribed. Some hands are suppler than others, and there are also varied hand configurations. Opposite the 2nd finger is a good thumb placement, when you have a hand structure friendly to this configuration. In all cases, I would encourage that thumb placement be at least opposite or preferably somewhat below the 1st finger (if hand placement opposite 2nd finger is not realistic for your particular hand configuration). The role of the thumb, as much as possible, is to balance and support the hand for use of the other fingers. A comfortable vibrato also very much depends on positive thumb placement.

For playing cello or bass, it would be great to have the thumb grow in a place that would balance the whole hand. This would mean the thumb would grow out of the area of the hand just opposite the 2nd and 3rd fingers. It is the balance of the hand that we are trying to achieve with the best possible placement of the thumb. To complicate matters, balance for the 4th finger ideally requires different thumb support than does the 1st or 2nd finger. When vibrating in slow passages, some relocation of the thumb to favor the finger being used for vibrato may allow for more comfort and flexibility. This practice is not always possible and will be governed by the tempo and length of notes being played.

At this point, it is necessary to mention that all fingers used in performing on the string should be arched. There is considerable excess tension in the use of flat (non-arched) fingers. All one has to do to demonstrate this is to press the string down with arched fingers (playing *on meaty pads* just below fingertips). Then try playing with straight, "locked" finger joints. Feel the increased tension in the uncurved finger joints. This excess tension causes the physically reactive behavior to be less agile and slower in response.

Note that musically, finger function is quite related to percussion sticks and mallets. In rapid passages, the fingers will drum on the string very rhythmically. Thus it is logical in warm-up practice period to have a few (short) simple rhythmic finger exercises. Trill practice can be a part of this process. Note the rhythm of your fingers in these exercises, but do not exaggerate by pounding too hard, as this can cause the fingers to be lifted too high. The higher the finger is lifted, the longer it takes to go up and down between notes; therefore, monitor how high fingers have to be lifted to achieve the rhythmic pulsation of the fingers. Fingers should not have to be lifted very much in order for them drum rhythmically on the string. (See "Trill, Finger, and Shifting Exercises," p. 77).

The Shifting Process

Always be aware that it is the arm that moves the left hand to wherever it needs to be on the fingerboard, very similar to a train carrying passengers from one place to another. The fingers are the wheels of the train and they glide along the track (strings) without brakes on (there's contact but no excess pressure). While the weight of the train causes heavy contact with the track, we only want a moderate contact with our track (strings), thus avoiding undue friction (tension) while shifting. The arm does the shifting, while the hand maintains a relatively relaxed contact with string. Full braking (pressure) takes place only when you have reached your destination (new position). This should guide all shifting, even in thumb position. To reiterate, use very modest pressure while shifting only applying full pressure when arriving at the note (destination). Excess pressure during the shifting process will result in moving the hand against the resistance of your locked brakes (unnecessary resistance and tension).

SHIFTING INTO THUMB POSITION

Many double bassists shift into thumb position with minimum preparation. This results in delayed preparatory maneuvering, usually occurring during the process of shifting rather than just before the shift. To get the gist of this process, assume the arm/hand position of a 2nd-finger B-flat in thumb position (using the fingering configuration of Thumb-1-2). Slide this whole mechanism back (without any alteration of hand/arm position), so that the thumb ends up on a D (in third position). Now slide back up to 2nd finger on B-flat, maintaining this thumb position while shifting back and forth. Do this several times and note how relaxed this is compared to the usual way of shifting into thumb position.

One will achieve a great deal of added comfort in shifting to thumb position by preparing as much of the thumb position (hand/arm shaping) as possible before the shift. The sequence: with the 2nd or 4th finger on pitch that precedes the thumb position shift, lift the arm so that the thumb comes from behind the neck to rest on top of the string. Now shift into thumb position as if you were almost shifting from one thumb position placement to another. Your shift will be made on the thumb, as well as 1st and 2nd fingers, and will feel very much like sledding down the string. We have thus accomplished the elimination of unnecessary maneuvering during the shift. This process is much the same as shifting from one thumb position to another, eliminating all changes of physical reshaping during the shift.

Practice scales extending thumb position backward, at least to where you place thumb on the lowest E or even D on the G string. You will find this use of fingerings in the Scales section of this book, on the pages with 2- and 3-octave scales. Some players have extended thumb position even below this and play some passages with an ease that defies traditional left-hand usage.

Ah Yes, Vibrato

Those who are having vibrato problems are most likely focusing on the wrong part of the anatomy for responsibility of the vibrato motion. It is the semi-rotation or, more correctly, undulation of the arm that controls the vibrato. It is not the hand or the wrist. The contact finger on the string is merely a pivot point for the undulating arm. It is the speed (and width) of the arm motion that controls the speed of the vibrato. Vibrato is nothing more than the undulating arm hinged on a pivot point (the finger) that causes the rocking up and down on the string. The arm motion causes the finger to pivot, or rock, on the string creating the sound of vibrato. The speed and width of the vibrato are created by the width and speed of the arm's undulations. Working to control these factors can allow you to achieve the vibrato that best pleases your ear. Our brains are not unlike computers; once they are programmed, they have to be deprogrammed. The brain is very resistant to changing programs (learned behavior) and requires time and focus to change habits, which is essentially "reprogramming." It will, for this reason, take time and effort to re-train any negative habits used to produce a vibrato or any other physical aspect of playing.

There is no hand vibrato for the bass, and even what is called "hand vibrato" on other string instruments usually involves more than hand alone. If you observe the process carefully, you will note some upper string players with vibratos that look locked in place or rigid. They vibrate this way because they either don't understand

Critical Analysis of Physical Performance Techniques

the science of the physical motion required or have never been properly taught the physics of vibrato. Listen carefully to vibratos on all the string instruments and note which type enhances the tone more desirably and sounds more consistent.

Vibrato speed should vary from one register to the other. If you listen keenly, you will note vibrato speeds can result in an unsatisfactory tonal experience when improperly created. It can sound too fast or too slow or may sound good in one register but not another. There are really different speeds and widths required for a good sounding vibrato. A proper vibrato on the E-string of the bass will not suit playing in thumb position on the G string. The thumb position vibrato will require a faster, narrower vibrato than a vibrato on the low E string. Generally, passages in the upper register require a faster vibrato than those in the lower registers. The intensity of a passage will also determine the speed/intensity of a vibrato.

What does this mean? Obviously, it requires us to vibrate faster and slower, wider and narrower, depending on the register in which we are playing and the intensity of the passage being performed. This requires investigative practice, as does the whole process of vibrato. How and when can we practice this? How do we find the least complicated materials where we can focus our primary attention on practicing vibrato? What I suggest here will be sacrilege to many. The answer is that scales present a perfect vehicle for vibrato practice in all registers, using notes of longer and shorter duration and different dynamics. Scales are the least complex pitch combinations, which allow for concentration without the complexity of passages with intricate fingerings.

Begin by practicing a rhythmic vibrato. Choose a comfortable speed of vibrato, and in the beginning, keep the same speed all the way through the scale. You may not find this comfortable, but it is part of the process for achieving control. Control the speed by counting the pulsations of the vibrato. These pulsations are easiest to count if you divide your thinking/listening into groupings of four. One need not really count 1-2-3-4, but one can easily feel the pulsation of four just as one would feel the pulsation of the repeated eighth-note Gs in the fifth bar of Mozart's "Eine Kleine Nachtmusik." You are probably feeling a pulse of two or four eighth notes but certainly not a pulse of a single eighth note or eight eighth notes. As you practice the scale, make sure the same number of vibrato pulsations is present for each note in the scale. It will be a challenge to control similar speeds in the lower positions, rather than the thumb position, but it can be done. Remember the speed of the undulation of the left arm is what is controlling the speed and width of your vibrato. Use it as the focal mechanism for vibrato control.

Once you are comfortably able to control one vibrato speed, start practicing other speeds by increasing the tempo of the undulating arm or decreasing the speed of the arm. In order to have an enhancing vibrato, one needs to control various speeds. Different intensities of music require different speeds of vibrato, as do different registers of pitch. This is something some singers fail to accomplish, and thus they sound musically ungainly in certain registers (especially true when the vibrato is too slow and wide in the upper register). When that happens you can actually hear the vibrato as a wobbling pitch rather than a technique that enhances musical sound. On the other hand, this same vibrato speed may sound quite in order in the middle or lower register, as those registers usually work better with a somewhat slower vibrato. Make vibrato a flexible part of your playing. A proper vibrato is an essential part of our tonal and musical efforts.

When this technical part of the vibrato process becomes comfortable and somewhat habitual, start practicing a continuous vibrato. This means the vibrato does not stop when you change pitches, change to a different finger, or change bow direction. You will notice that the vibrato often disappears at the end of a note when one prepares to change pitch or shift. This can be controlled. First try continuous vibrato by playing 1st finger to 4th finger (in one position, while still counting pulsations). The solution is to keep the arm rhythmically undulating without cessation while changing the finger being played, shifting, or changing bow direction. The process is easier when slurring while playing in one position, so start by slurring the 1st finger to the 4th finger. Keep the vibrato going by concentrating on the arm motion continuing (still counting the pulsations). After some trials you will find you can keep vibrating through the changing of fingers, as the left arm does not have to stop undulating because you are changing fingers within one position. This is all merely mental training and retraining physical habits. When teaching, I find that anyone who can successfully vibrate can also learn continuous vibrato.

The next step is to practice this continuation of vibrato while changing bow. Again, the concentration is on the continuity of the left arm rhythmically continuing to vibrate (undulate) regardless of the right arm changing bow or the left hand changing fingers in the same position. When you achieve the continuity of vibrato while slurring two notes in one position, it is quite clear that for the left hand, there really is no difference when the right arm is changing bow rather than slurring (while using the basic 1st-to-4th-finger exercise in one position).

This concentration on vibrato now has to go further than playing in one position. The next logical, least complicated application is scales. I know there is a shudder out there about practicing vibrato in scales. The basic reasoning for scales without vibrato is clear, but it is partially flawed. Using vibrato is usually constant in a string player's performances. If vibrato is not practiced methodically, as should all other aspects of technical and musical performance, then how does it become a controlled and positive part of one's performing abilities? I understand the practice of playing scales without vibrato for the purpose of achieving pure and unadulterated intonation. However, including the practice of vibrato also helps establish positive intonation for performing with vibrato. It is an essential aspect of one's ability to play in tune. Lack of a properly controlled vibrato quite negatively affects tonal results. In the end, one plays in tune because one has practiced playing in tune if one has the aural perception for intonation. A sleeping ear cannot be awakened to pitch accuracy if an innate aural ability does not exist. The level of accuracy in intonation achieved is based on one's developed innate ability to be able to discriminate intonation. None of these comments have to do with what we describe as "perfect pitch." That is another aural element, but not at all essential for proper discrimination of intonation.

When some control over the mechanical/physical process of vibrating is achieved, practicing vibrato in scales should mimic the quality of vibrato used in solo or orchestral performance. This means that the vibrato speed should complement the pitch register being used.

In solo performance, make sure the vibrato you use colors the passage appropriately. Intense passages will require a faster vibrato than more relaxed passages. To properly color and interpret the music we perform, all aspects of our performance techniques will need to be adjusted to the musical demands of the moment. Vibrato is just one of them.

The Bow Arm:
BODY (STANCE, LEVERAGE),
ARM (POSITION, FUNCTION),
HAND (HIERARCHY, FUNCTION)

In assuming any body stance related to a specific activity, it is essential to be properly balanced for that activity. Think of athletic stances, like that for the golfer, the boxer, the batter, the catcher, the shortstop, the tennis player, and then those for the violinist, the cellist and certainly, the double bassist. What are we preparing for: bowing, shifting, sharp bow attacks, thumb position, pizzicato, or a long number of bars' rest? All of the stances for double bass mentioned take some adjustment in body stance or positioning. Some of the athletic stances mentioned above are not wholly divorced from the double bass stance. Most of them provide a stance that is preparing to send energy forward, in the case of the boxer, the tennis player, the golfer, and the batter. We also need to provide a stance that allows positive body leverage. The leverage required even changes from down-bow to up-bow. Although there are various stances in use, the correct stance will give you the greatest ability to shift your weight/leverage as needed and to deliver the required energy to the act being performed. So far, I've been referring to the standing position primarily, but there are equally important implications for playing in the seated position.

Bowing is perhaps the biggest benefactor from proper stance. Although we can't walk around like a solo violinist does, we are not static in our stance. Be aware of the body adjustments needed to play on the G string versus the E string. Note the body's accommodations for playing in thumb position versus first position. We need to learn how to use the body to our best advantage for all the various maneuvers performing on the bass requires. These body movements need to be no more than absolutely necessary, but enough to provide the proper leverage and access for bowing and left arm/hand maneuverability.

There is really no totally comfortable position when playing an instrument the size of the double bass. Most of us are smaller in structure and height than what we should be to maintain a completely healthy physical stature on so large an instrument. This becomes more apparent the older we get. The constant leaning toward the instrument we have to do in order to achieve the needed leverage causes us various struc-

Critical Analysis of Physical Performance Techniques

tural ills (i.e. round shoulders, back discomfort, scoliosis, tendonitis, arm ailments, neck muscle problems, etc.). However, I don't think these dilemmas would make most of us give up our double basses in exchange for another musical instrument. Bassists 6'2" or taller, with larger hands, do not to fall into the same category as the rest of us. They approach the measurements that should be minimal for playing a double bass.

I insert here some advice for all of us to heed if we wish to maintain healthy structures, even in later life. Consult with trainers, therapists, or doctors in sports medicine and learn about various exercises that will not only keep you fit but counteract the negative physical behavior required to play our instrument. Ironically, the smallest member of the string family also takes its toll physically. Violinists and violists are always turned more in one direction than the other. One arm is farther up than the other. Their heads are not naturally aligned. They, too, experience structural problems as time progresses. They, too, can help themselves by doing proper exercises, restricting extended practicing before feeling the strain or pain of overtaxing muscles and tendons. Just relaxing by taking a five-minute rest before feeling the strain will help prevent aching muscles. We all know from experience how long we can practice before the feeling of discomfort begins to be felt. Don't wait to reach that point. Each time we play and go beyond that point of muscular and tendon stress, we are setting the stage for the structural afflictions that string players experience, learning too late that some damage has been done and that increased sensitivity to strain and pain now exist. Maintaining a normally healthy physique, regularly doing proper exercises to strengthen body parts we abuse, and reacting to what your body is telling you about structural exhaustion while playing can lead to a more trouble-free physical comfort at all ages. Add the process of massaging the arms while taking the five-minute rest period. It helps circulation and seems to relax the muscles.

Standing and sitting while playing both have their advantages and disadvantages. I will first discuss the position of standing. In a standing position, I prefer a stance a bit similar to a boxer's (left foot modestly forward), allowing my torso to shift and provide leverage for the bow and left arm. By contrast, try standing straight up, with feet together and body erect, without bending, and then attempt to play with a full sound. Note how distant your bow arm feels from the body. This restricted posture will give you the sensation of using a bow arm with greatly reduced available power and leverage. Unfortunately, some leaning of the body forward (toward the bass) has to take place to allow body leverage to go in the direction of the physical effort being made.

Use both arms/hands and press down on a horizontal surface like a desk or tabletop. Lean into the effort and feel your body energy being transmitted and supported by the hands and arms. Get your back into it, as they say. You should experience your body being totally involved in this effort, including legs and stance. Take note of your total body position used to achieve this act. A similar leverage and total involvement is needed for playing the double bass, and a stance must be found for this as well. Although our level of effort is significantly modified to the requirements of what we are playing, a totally integrated body is needed for physical performance. Proper leverage is most essential for the energy and balance required for bowing.

Critical Analysis of Physical Performance Techniques

The purpose of a proper stance is to gain the fullest access to the instrument possible; to feel body and arms involved in a coordinated effort, very much like you would be if you were sawing a piece of wood. Imagine using your body leverage and weight to provide leverage for the sawing arm. We need similar body-arm cooperation when bowing a string instrument.

Watch a violin section and note how bowing behavior varies. Some play as if they think bowing is an obligation primarily of the hand and forearm, while others show their generation of energy through a more complete arm/body coordination. A well-trained bow arm is a graceful-looking integration of body, arm, hand, and fingers. It is beautiful to watch a well-oiled bow arm backed by correct application of body leverage. Bowing is not an act restricted to any one part of the anatomy. It is not primarily an obligation of the hand. It is an integration of all moving parts supported by proper body leverage. It is the arm that moves the hand; the hand that carries the fingers that respond to the feeling of the resistance created by the bow hair being pushed or pulled across the string.

Fingers are certainly very important and are responsible for much of the subtlety in bowing and for the special mobility required in strokes like spiccato, tremolo, etc. They are also part of the cure for the faulty bow change, if subtly used and not exaggerated.

Summarizing, there needs to be a proper stance, body preparation, and anticipation of the act (such as your preparation in anticipation of reaching for a door handle when opening a door). The process gradually becomes instinctive with practice and experience. Practicing and evaluating the results of our repeated efforts to anticipate the balance, motion and energy we will need for a given physical musical effort will eventually result in instinctively being balanced for the physical use of self in performing. This is what practice should be for. We learn through *conscious* experimental repetitions of passages, seeking proper body usage, body balance, fingering, bow length, bow speed, bow pressure, bow placement, shifting accuracy, vibrato speed, etc.

It is truly a very complex process we need to conquer to play in tune, to phrase musically, to play rhythmically, to produce a beautiful sound, and to vibrate correctly for every specific musical level of intensity. Playing indeed is an intricate science as well as an inspired artful effort we use to express ourselves and entertain others.

A beautiful bow stroke pulls and pushes sound out of the string with visual grace. The successful integration of body, arm, hand, and fingers create this visual art of motion.

Exaggerated use of body motion is generally criticized and probably with some justification, but a string player who is frozen in place or remains immobile will not achieve proper leverage. If a choice needs to be made, I will forgive the performer with exaggerated physical expressiveness that provides for positive use of body leverage, but not the one who inhibits leverage, causing negative musical results through of a lack of inertia.

Bowing, if properly executed, is not solely the effort of the arm, wrist, hand, and fingers. Observing violin soloists who are performing while standing, one usually sees

Critical Analysis of Physical Performance Techniques

the body's motion, some leg movement, and impressively active bow strokes all creating the balance and leverage and energy that are integral to the act of performing. Study the bow arm and the consequences of the body and leg motions you see in a live performance. Playing does not start at the shoulder joints just involving the arms and hands. Athletically, a well-tuned string player has a great deal of the energy for bowing that comes from the rest of the body, including from the legs (even in a seated position). It is the same use of body made by a baseball batter, a pitcher, or by any athletic effort. Notice how visual the total body efforts of the fine violin, viola, and cello soloists are. Observing a fine string quartet allows seeing this energetic effort taking place with the other string players. I don't mean to ignore the fine artists who play double bass, as similar examples of positive physical behavior will of course be observed in their efforts as well.

I use the examples of the violinists and violists because they can move around more freely, unrestricted by an end pin. Their visual efforts can be more easily seen. Their relative body and arm motions are even more apparent and impressive when considering the size of their instrument. However, it is not the size of the instrument that is most involved here but the length of the bow and bow stroke required. Their bows are about as long as ours, even though their instruments are miniscule by comparison. The result, of course, is a need for great energy and motion in the bow arms, which is visually more equal to ours than one would expect.

Consciousness of bowing should first be an awareness of the body's preparation (similar to preparing to take a deep breath), then the awareness of moving the arm from the shoulder (with energy from both body and arm). The arm moves, carrying the hand with it, and when the bow touches the string, the hand and fingers react with anticipation to the resistance (between the bow and the string). This is where we feel the pull of the arm against the hand and fingers, allowing the wrist and fingers to respond to the feeling of contact and resistance of the string. For bow changes immediately before the change, we anticipate the change of direction and the resistance factor, cushioning the motion of the bow hair that is changing direction by the consciously controlled use of the wrist and fingers and by modifying the arm weight/pressure. If properly activated, the precise timing and use of the wrist, fingers, and arm weight can act as shock absorbers for the tonal disruption at the change of bow. We all agree that in *legato* playing we want to eliminate as much excess sound of the bow change as possible. There is, however, one important aspect of the bow change we must rethink and conquer. The natural and common instinct is to change bow as quickly as possible. This most often results in a speeding up of the bow hair at the bow change, causing a momentary surge in sound rather than a cushioning of the bow change. This is common on all bowed instruments. Given constant pressure, speeding up the hair increases volume, while slowing down decreases volume. Our effort really needs to balance the three factors that go into creating sound on a string instrument: speed, pressure, and resistance. The factor of the bow hair's speed is obvious. Pressure is a result of the weight the arm transmits through the hand and fingers to the bow. Resistance starts with the tension of the string, which reacts to the speed of, and the pressure on, the bow. Resistance varies with the pressure applied to the bow by the bow arm. It also varies according to the pitch register in which one is playing and correspondingly where the bow is placed between the bridge and the fingerboard. To give the illusion of a smooth bow change, we need to decrease speed and pressure, thus decreasing resistance and actually momentarily decreasing volume. With practice, trying to slow the stroke for a split second and lightening up pressure at bow changes can create the illusion of a more connected bow stroke. The truth is that in changing direction of the bow, there has to be a momentary (hopefully inaudible) cessation in the sound. Our effort is to create the illusion that there is continuity in the sound and that the quality and quantity of sound remains constant during the bow change. "Flipping" the bow when changing bow direction increases bow speed, which causes a surge in volume, defeating the possibility of an inaudible bow change. Eliminating the result of this flip can be achieved by decreasing pressure for a split second at bow changes, and by decreasing bow speed. Since changing habits requires time and patience, expect to master this process only after you have been working at it for a number of months.

The importance of being aware that the arms are the main and initial source of motion cannot be overly stressed. Certainly hands and fingers have their own significant and complex roles to play, but they go nowhere without the arms and are primarily responders to the motions of the arm and resistance of the string. The role of the hand and fingers always seems more obvious to us, as they are the source of feeling or contact. They are most closely associated with the objects we hold and use when performing. For this reason, we too often lose awareness of the great importance that the arm has in creating the proper bow stroke, vibrato, or shift.

Sound Production

SPEED, PRESSURE, RESISTANCE, BOW ANGLE (TILT)

Although bow speed, pressure, and resistance have already been discussed, there is still more to consider. In determining bow speed, there are of course a variety of bow speeds we can use. If we were playing a forte passage and wanted a more flowing sound rather than an intense sound we would use more bow (more flow). If we wanted a more intense sound, we would use more pressure and less bow, while moving the bow hair closer to the bridge, thus increasing resistance. The exact area on the string for bow placement depends on the exact sound required, the characteristics of your bass, the type of strings you are using, and the register being employed, but in all cases you will be moving toward the bridge for more intensity and in the opposite direction for less intensity. Playing closer to the bridge creates more resistance, which usually causes one to use more energy (pressure), also requiring a slower bow speed. If the bow speed did not diminish in this circumstance, the sound would probably break resulting in scratching. This is only one illustration of how speed, pressure, and resistance are involved. These factors are always involved in bowing. If there is a problem in producing a satisfactory sound, it will be the result of the imbalance of these three factors.

Critical Analysis of Physical Performance Techniques

The factor I often see violated is the awareness of resistance. When playing the lower B-flat on the G string, versus a B-flat an octave higher on the G string, the resistance factor changes. Basically, by shortening the vibrating string (when playing high B-flat) string tension (resistance) increases, and conversely for the lower B-flat. When changing pitch on one string, you are actually lengthening or shortening the string. The higher the pitch one plays, the shorter the vibrating string length becomes. This changes the center of the vibrating string as well. Thus, if you bow in the same place (closer to the fingerboard) for the high B-flat as you do for the low B-flat, you will actually be playing closer to the center of the (shortened) string, which decreases resistance. A relative distance from the vibrating center of the string must be maintained by the bow when playing in all registers to successfully control the quality of sound. Moving the bow closer to the bridge for the high B-flat will compensate for change in resistance and help provide balance to the quality of sound. Bow placement on the string needs to consider the three factors: speed, pressure, and resistance, which are greatly influenced by the register of the string you are using and the quality and quantity of sound that needs to be satisfied.

As you no doubt have noted, playing on the E string usually requires a slower bow speed and more pressure to produce a tone than matching tonal qualities for a note played in the lower range of the G string. You may have instinctively already adjusted speed and pressure to compensate for the difference in resistance between higher and lower strings and higher and lower registers, in order to produce the desired tonal result. This process goes on constantly as we are playing throughout the range of the instrument. Being aware of these changing elements for producing a sound on a string instrument can improve the quality of sound and allow you to control tonal coloring for desired musical expressiveness. A very simple thought that says much is that forte cannot mean playing closer to the fingerboard and piano does not mean placing the bow closer to the bridge.

To demonstrate how we should be engaging the whole self in sound production, again think of the process of sawing a piece of wood. Consider your bow the saw and place your bass somewhat horizontally, so that you can actually saw with your bow. Now really bear down and saw with the bow in the usual bowing area, noticing your total involvement of body (back), arms, stance (legs), and how you have shaped yourself for the process of sawing. A similar total involvement (highly refined of course) must be part of playing a string instrument. We are constantly rebalancing ourselves when standing in order to play on the different strings and different registers of the instrument. Balance may be very subtle but is as essential to playing an instrument as it is in sports. Think of a baseball shortstop or tennis player who has to be ready to go in any position to catch or hit the ball. We need to be that versatile in our body, fingering, and bowing in order to be in control of the next sound, the next shift, and the next fingering with the most comfort and success.

Sitting presents a frustration of achieving real comfort with an instrument the size of the double bass. There are numerous positions used in playing while seated and there are probably arguments for many of these positions. The practices include: left foot on the floor, left foot on a rung of the stool, both feet on the floor, or possibly

Critical Analysis of Physical Performance Techniques

both feet on the lowest rung of stool. None of these positions are perfect, and again it is because of the size of instrument we play. When sitting while playing, note this bit of advice. If you sit with your left foot on a rung of stool, do not use the highest rung. You are causing restriction of the circulation and cramping your left leg, thus abusing thigh muscles and tendons. Over the years, you will probably develop discomfort in that leg as a result of long periods in this cramped position. Using the lowest rung of the stool or having special bass stools with adjustable foot rests for the left leg is a much better physical compromise. Try not to stretch out the right leg unnecessarily, as that also can cause eventual leg discomfort. Maintain a comfortably bent knee. A good sitting position will allow proper body mobility, comfortable access to your instrument, and a body position that doesn't strain your arms, legs, or torso. Primarily accommodate the bow arm, which has less flexibility for achieving proper leverage and body mobility. There is a little more leeway with the left arm, which has a bit more room for adaptability. You do, however, want the fingerboard to be close enough and angled enough so that you are not unnecessarily reaching around the neck for access. Note that a bass with the upper portion (neck and scroll) excessively angled away from the player requires a longer reach for the bow arm to access the strings. A too-upright position for the bass is a detriment to the left arm, which will have to reach (stretch) out farther to contact the neck.

There have been all kinds of efforts made to achieve better playing positions: the long end pin, the bent end pin, and sitting on a very low stool are examples of these. The search for a better position confirms that the instrument itself presents a challenge to finding the ideal position. In the end, keep in mind what you are trying to accomplish: bowing comfort, left arm comfort, body comfort, balance, and integrity Experiment until you find the compromise that works the best. As already commented, I suspect that perfection of comfort may not exist for those of us who are not at least 6'2" or taller, with longer arms and bigger hands, yet we must strive to achieve the most accommodating playing position for our personal body proportions.

More Thoughts on Performance Practices

Why do we tilt our bows?

It seems that in this process of being analytical, it should be meaningful to explore related issues such as why *do* we tilt our bows?

For those who have tried exploring sound, playing with "flat hair" versus using a "tilted" bow, I am sure you have found that even though the difference is not earth-shaking, there is some added clarity and/or edge in the sound when using a tilted bow.

Several technical and scientific things are going on. When using flat hair and a bow that is absolutely at right angles to the string, you are creating pretty much the same pressure on all of the hairs, which in turn press down on the string equally over the width or span of the hairs. You are actually also inhibiting the vibration of the string over the total span of the hair. When tilting the bow, the pressure put on the span of hair is greater on one side than the other. This results in a smaller area on the bridge side of the string being inhibited from vibrating by the bow hair. In other words, tilting the bow causes more of the pressure to be concentrated on the portion of the bow hair closer to the fingerboard, while it decreases pressure on the side of the bow hair closer to the bridge. This decrease in pressure on one side of the bow hair allows the strings to vibrate more freely under that portion of the bow hair. This creates somewhat more edge or centering of the tone, because the string is not inhibited from vibrating freely for the *full* width of the bow hair. The audible difference will not be dramatic, but it exists. On the other hand, we need the strength and resistance of a sufficient number of hairs to produce sound and provide support for the many articulations and tonal qualities we wish to produce. By experimenting objectively, you can determine what angle of bow tilt will provide the best results. The amount of tilt used will be determined by the volume and quality of the sound desired (required). For instance, when a heavy fortissimo is called for, you will be applying more pressure over more of the width of the bow hair to support all the additional weight you are now placing on the bow.

Thankfully, bow makers and performers throughout history gradually resolved the question of span and thickness of bow hair needed for optimum performance qualities. However, as you can tell from the different bows you have tried, making an excellent playing bow is, even today, beyond pure science, or we would not have to search so carefully for an ideal bow.

For a more complete discussion on the desirable playing qualities of a double bass bow, see "Purchasing a Fine Bow."

How Much Input of Energy is Too Much?

SHOULD WE STRIVE FOR SIMILAR TONAL INTENSITIES AS PRODUCED BY VIOLINISTS, VIOLISTS, AND CELLISTS?

Double bass playing is a musical effort unlike playing the other string instruments. Even under normal performance conditions, creating a similar range of colors and dynamics on the double bass presents a greater challenge than on other instruments. Our strings are much heavier and more resistant to producing sound. Our bows, however, are not proportionately heavier than violin or cello bows. If they were, they would be too heavy and inflexible to use. Much more control and effort is required for the double bassist to equal the color and clarity of tone of the other orchestral string instruments.

Clean, clear, precise, and in-tune playing are goals with which we cannot disagree. However, to achieve these goals, many of us have given up our dynamic range, as "digging in" has become undesirable because it is claimed to obscure clarity and affect quality of sound. We have accepted the premise that auditioning committees are less interested in the musical expressiveness, imaginative phrasing, or range of tonal colors bassists can produce, and more concerned with whether one can play cleanly and with good intonation. As a result, the range of *forte* and *piano* is often so limited that a monotone of expressiveness seems to be the norm.

Interestingly enough, in solo playing, where we could take advantage of playing with a greater range of dynamics and color, I find the same relatively monotone dynamics and musical expressiveness. How do we engage ourselves in the dynamics of **pp**, **p**, **mp**, **mf**, **f**, and **ff**, if our usual practice includes only playing **p**, **mf**, and a modest **f**?

Obviously all string players need to play with tonal, rhythmic, and intonation accuracy. However, there is a need for a renaissance in double bass playing that includes all of the foregoing but also includes musical dynamics and tonal expressiveness, which make us sound like equal members of the string family. There are outstanding bassists like Karr, Petracchi, Stoll, and others we all admire who play with full dynamic ranges and expressiveness. Why do we admire them and then go back to the mediocrity of *mezzo-forte* expressiveness? Inhibition is not a way to make music.

In order to achieve the level of performance quality our colleagues in the string family attain, we must learn to extend our dynamic range and utilize the expressive tonal colors and phrasing they employ. It is not a new venture, but one that is currently being employed by many fine contemporary soloists and orchestral bassists. I believe the phrase "seek and ye shall find," is appropriate for the needed renaissance. To listen to the recordings of Stern, Oistrakh, Rostrapovich, Karr, and Petracchi, and not be inspired to emulate their beauty of tonal expressiveness is to have cheated ourselves of a full musical existence. This same beauty of tonal sculpturing needs to be part of our effort, whether for the purpose of solo playing or orchestral performance. It is not something new. It exists. Listen to the Leipzig Gewandhaus Orchestra or the Concertgebauw. Picture yourself performing with the Emerson Quartet. Monotone music-making is a failure to have enjoyed musical performance to the fullest.

Developing an Automatically Responsive Bow Arm and Left Hand/Arm

THROUGH THE USE OF SCALES, ARPEGGIOS, AND BOWINGS

If you are going to develop your bowing and left-hand technique so that they are ready to deal with most of the challenges that music presents, you have to be *trained* to respond at will to the many bowing and left-hand demands. Being ready to respond to the challenges music presents means having studied and mastered all the predictable bow strokes and left hand/arm patterns.

What is going to allow for the most concentration and presentation of these patterns in their basic forms? Scales (major, minor, and chromatic) and arpeggios. Nothing is as fundamental to use as these vehicles, which relate to most conventionally written music. Most music is either stepwise or employs larger intervals (usually related to arpeggio patterns). One should be trained to automatically have the skills to respond to passages that are scale-like or arpeggiated, which permeate the greatest bulk of our literature.

Through the daily practice of all types of scales, arpeggios, and bowing (in scales), we create a behavioral pattern, which is mentally stored, allowing immediate learned responses to most traditionally written music. When we admire someone's ability to sight-read, we are seeing and hearing the result of these quick mental responses to the visual instructions on the page. A quick mental response comes from the developed ability to physically and mentally react to patterns that the brain recognizes and has been programmed to control. It is not the brain that is like a computer, but the computer that is like the brain. The brain can reason; the computer cannot. Both the computer and the brain may be infinite in their ability to store information. Both the computer and the brain have to be programmed in order to respond to specific commands and provide solutions, whether they are physical or intellectual.

Constant practicing of scales programs the left hand in all the various diatonic patterns. Adding the practice of arpeggios establishes use of the left hand in movement and fingering for intervals of thirds and fourths. It is essential that fingering patterns for both scales and arpeggios allow for the most efficient use of the left arm/hand. Efficient can also mean the most facile, thus allowing the fastest accurate motion of the left arm/hand. As an example, think of the last movement of Mozart's Symphony no. 35 (see p.89). One would not think of playing those famous audition passages without open strings. Why? Not using open strings requires extra maneuvering and stopping of the strings, which would cause many of us not to be able to play this passage (or others) at the required tempos. While many teachers request only closed (stopped) strings when practicing scales, it is also essential to learn to play scales with the most facile fingering, which unquestionably means playing them with open strings. One should also include playing slow scales with closed strings. This may help intonation and programs the brain to find second position on the E, A, and D strings. Of course, the stopped string may be tonally preferable when playing slow melodic passages, but it is as essential if not more essential to learn to play scales at moderate and fast tempos with open strings for the purpose of establishing finger patterns that will allow more facility in faster tempos.

One plays in tune because his or her ears are trained for pitch discrimination and have acquired a tactile memory for the location of pitches through organized practicing. Some of this learning has been through the osmosis of being immersed in musical sound and by mentally absorbing the sound of positive intonation. The mental hearing/listening process is then awake and responding. Others who possess the innate ability to properly discriminate intonation but have not awakened or trained this potential usually remain less sensitive to intonation discrimination. Playing open or closed strings only in scales is not a cure for the less sensitive ear. The argument for playing scales with closed strings bears only so much fruit. It must not stand in the way of students learning to maneuver rapidly in scales and in the process developing fingering patterns that prepare one to master musical passages that require a great deal of dexterity. Playing scales using open strings for dexterity is essential. It is a fingering practice we all use for scale-like passages in Mozart's Symphony no. 35, Fourth movement (p.89) and many other orchestral works demanding the rapid movement of the left hand/arm.

The stepwise sequence of pitches comes in various patterns, and it is necessary to develop significant dexterity in the various patterns found in major, minor (both forms), and chromatic scales. They all contain unique patterns of their own, and each has their own programs for the brain. Arpeggios have their own sequence of patterns and need to be mastered first in major and minor, and subsequently in many of the other harmonic forms. Fingerings for all of these patterns must be the most maneuverable. Tempo will usually determine when to make appropriate use of open strings.

The same basic need for programming the brain is present for all the various maneuvers of the bow arm. Most of these maneuvers are part of the various basic bowing strokes. Each basic bowing stroke usually has a program of its own that needs to be learned. The bowings include slurring, spiccato, staccato, hooked bowings (dotted eighth followed by sixteenth), and bowings that are combinations of two basic strokes. The latter can also create a completely new physical challenge.

Programming the above left and right hand/arm patterns to be automatic responses (programs stored by the brain) enables a player to use the most basic and advanced techniques as tools to construct and perfect musical passages. Neglected basic techniques should not become stumbling blocks. Once in command of these techniques, one will usually recognize that the difficulty is not unique to that passage but is actually a universal technique already in one's toolbox. For example, a hooked bowing occurs in various forms in Schubert Ninth Symphony's first, second, and fourth movement (see p. 95); Mozart Symphony no. 41, fourth movement (p.94); Beethoven Symphony no. 7, first movement (p.80); Weber's *Euryanthe Overture* (p.100); and innumerable other places. These passages depend on mastering the hooked bowing; recognizing this is helpful to successfully performing these passages. Although these orchestral examples don't all look the same, the basic bowing technique is the same.

How to Problem Solve

In order to solve any performance problem, first you have to identify the problem. Is it a bowing, the left hand, or a string-crossing problem, or perhaps a passage that presents problems for more than one performance technique?

We have already discussed the passage in Mozart's Fortieth Symphony that occurs in the last movement (p. 92). This is a passage that presents problems for both bowing and the left hand. Listen carefully to your playing or that of a colleague. Note first if the bowing is very articulate, as previously discussed. Until the bow clearly articulates the slur and the two separate strokes in each half bar, there is no way for the left hand/arm to make the passage sound clearly. Assuming the bowing is resolved and the passage is still not clear, the next thing to determine is if the left arm is getting the fingers to the notes in perfect rhythm. Usually, if there is a left arm/hand problem in this passage, you will find it is the arm that is usually late in getting the hand from the C back to the A. It's also possible that the C is held too long, preventing the arm from making the shift back to A quickly enough.

First try playing the first five notes of the passage exactly in time. Use a metronome.

Let go of the C as soon as possible, so the arm does not have to pull (shift) against a C locked in place for a fraction of a second too long. Play the five-note sequence as many times as it takes to maintain perfect rhythm in fingers, bowing, and shifting. Now alternate by playing sequence at first down-bow, rhythmic pause, and then up-bow. Count a full measure of rest between playing up- and down-bow versions. When this process seems perfect, try and play the whole first bar plus the B-flat in the next bar. When this effort begins to bring success, add the second bar of the passage. Force the bow to maintain the tempo in the second bar. If you find the left hand falling behind, realize that it is not primarily the fingering that is falling behind but the arm, which has to change from the descending motion of the last shift in the first bar to the ascending motion that is required in the first half of the second bar. What I am saying is that if you could play all the required finger patterns of the passage in one position, you would discover the challenge was not really in the fingers but in the time required for shifting. To solve the passage, use the devices I have suggested or perhaps ideas of your own that will create more successful shifting of the left arm. However, the main purpose of all this is to analyze and identify the reasons a passage challenges your ability to play it successfully. Of course, we can only succeed up to the point that our basic skills have been developed. The Mozart is not a problem to be resolved by someone who has not studied long enough to develop the level of skills needed for the challenges of that passage. This passage is a challenge for most of us who have played double bass for many years. Realizing what the technical problem is that needs improvement helps us find more successful results.

The purpose of this analysis is to show you that learning how to play a challenging passage usually requires more than playing it through a hundred or more times, assuming learning will take place through repetition or osmosis. Repetition is in a way "blind" practicing. When the problem is not recognized, even if the passage gets better through repetition, one has not necessarily recognized the core of the problem. To perform the passage more successfully, one must focus on the playing technique that can be used to resolve the problem, as in other passages with the same core problem. One has to recognize the core problem in a passage in order to analyze the left-hand or bow maneuvers that create difficulty. Never practice blindly. Make every practice session one of solving and resolving technical problems. This will aid you with the many other passages involving similar problems or techniques. Analytical (aware) practicing will require much less time to achieve success than blind, repetitive workhorse practicing.

More problem solving will be discussed in the section on bowings related to orchestral excerpts.

Perfecting and Resolving Techniques
THROUGH USE OF SCALES, BOWINGS, ARPEGGIOS, AND SPECIAL EXERCISES

We are now at a point where we will interrupt the prose and explore the use of scales with bowings. They will be used as a means of establishing and/or refining basic and advanced techniques essential to the physical and intellectual control we must achieve to execute the music accurately and express our thoughts musically. The sections following scales and bowings also contain important related exercises and materials to challenge and enhance our performing abilities.

Everything we have learned to do, whether it is the act of walking or cycling, is a result of learning either through experimentation and practice, like walking, or via analytical instruction, as we receive for math, geometry, and yes, various athletic skills. Experimentation (trial and error) is usually a much longer process than learning through instruction from competent instructors.

The following scale, bowing, and musical exercises will provide a detailed analytical approach to mastering most of the skills required to perform the challenges of the printed page. Performing on a string instrument is made up of numerous programs for usage of one's self. Too much learning takes place by trial and error, often leading to inefficient and faulty "use of self." Practicing a passage one hundred times is not the efficient path to learning and control. Isolating the problem(s) in a passage and resolving the technique required to master the passage allows one to learn the passage and acquire a specific technique that, once mastered, will provide solutions for passages presenting the same technical challenge(s).

The greatest workshops for technical development and building a repertoire of techniques for most of music's challenges are scales with bowings and the other exercises found on the following pages. A physical and musical analysis will be given for examples presented in that section.

Scales

Choose a fingering for each scale that would be related to fingerings you would employ for playing rapid diatonic passages in that key. This dictates using open strings in order to establish the most maneuverable habit of fingering that translates to diatonic passages in the fast movements of orchestral and solo repertoire.

Scales should be played without repeating tonics. See examples 5 and 6 and note that the scale uses no repeated tonics and is replayed until the tonic again falls on the downbeat. In this example of slurring two notes, it takes playing through the scale twice to arrive with the tonic on the downbeat. Slurring three notes will require playing through the scale three times (in a 2-octave scale) to arrive with the tonic on the downbeat. These two examples provide all possible combinations of bowings and fingerings when slurring two or three notes (using a fixed set of fingerings). Each bowing will require playing through a scale as many times as it takes to arrive with tonic on the downbeat. In other words, we are allowing all the possible permutations between bow and fingering (using one set of scale fingerings) for any given key.

Perfection through practice does require repetition, but specifically while using playing habits that have been learned through analytical instruction. The use of scales allows the most basic and often-used technique of the left hand. There is no better or simpler approach to tactile accuracy (intonation) than scales, arpeggios, and chromatic scales. Scales are never boring when being used for accurately minute development of intonation, tonal qualities, ease of shifting, bowing articulations, volume control, and, yes, vibrato. One can become extremely articulate technically by mastering the following materials. There is no problem presented on the following pages that, if mastered, will not diminish or cease to be a problem when met in solo or orchestral music.

Proceed to the following section, *Essential Bowings to Use in Scales*. Starting on page 51, you will find several sets of fingerings for each scale in both 2 and 3 octaves. You may wish to explore these fingerings before deciding on the fingering you will choose for each scale.

(NOTE: In all the playing efforts you make, there are always three elements involved: bow speed, pressure and string resistance. Any variation in application of one or more of these elements will affect the resultant tonal qualities of your sound. Playing scales and arpeggios provides a perfect medium for tonal awareness. Staying sensitive to these elements and their effect on tonal results may encourage some rebalancing that enhances tonal results. Aural awareness is an essential guide to musical growth.)

PART 2

Perfecting Techniques through Employing Scales, Exercises, and Orchestral Excerpts

BOWINGS, SCALES, AND EXERCISES

Approach each bowing in a slow tempo concentrating on controlling tonal quality and accurate intonation. Do use and practice vibrato in the slower tempos. Strive to achieve a continuous vibrato as described in the section on vibrato. Play with a full but relaxed sound. Your effort for perfection in this section will carry over to your performance in most other musical challenges. In brief, play everything with a goal of doing it to the best of your ability, constantly working to improve that ability.

Use only one major or minor 2- or 3-octave scale with bowings per day. Include representation of several examples of bowings from Sustained Bowings, Slurred Bowings, Alternating Patterns, Hooked Bowings, and Spiccato. In addition concentrate on several examples of problematic bowings from 27–53. Also include the practice of arpeggios and the chromatic scale in the same tonality as the major or minor scale used for that day. Suggested scale and arpeggio fingerings can be found in Section II (p. 61).

You will note that some exercises have tempo markings. A dual marking indicates the range of tempos you should use for that exercise. It is obviously not practical to practice all bowing examples found on the following pages in a single practice period.

Perfecting Techniques through Employing Scales, Exercises, and Orchestral Excerpts

Essential Bowings to Use in Scales

GUIDE TO ABBREVIATIONS:
w.b. = whole bow
l.h. = lower half of bow
h.b. = half bow
u.h. = upper half of bow
m.b. = middle section of bow

Sustained Bowings

(Daily include examples 1, 2, 2a, plus 3 or 4)

The main objectives for these bowings are sustaining the quality and quantity of sound plus creating as indiscernible a bow change as possible. Use a full forte sound, but without forcing or tonal exaggeration. Concentrate on smooth bow changes using techniques discussed in the preceding section discussing bow changes. Bowings 1–2a should be played slowly, with full, connected strokes. Maintain a constant volume and work for as smooth and uninterrupted a bow change as possible. Do not lurch or increase bow speed at bow changes. Try to maintain a constant vibrato through (counting) regular pulsations. (Consult section on vibrato, if you need a refresher.)

1.
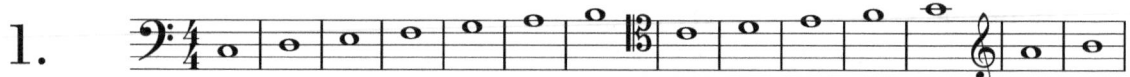

2.

Perfecting Techniques through Employing Scales, Exercises, and Orchestral Excerpts

Bowings 2a, 3, and 4 should start out andante and with each playing increase tempo speed, still striving for a full, even, legato sound with smooth bow changes. Bowing 4 will end up being played at a faster moving tempo, while maintaining a full sonority and legato bow change. Moderately exaggerate the length of the bow stroke, but without losing control of any aspects of sound production.

Perfecting Techniques through Employing Scales, Exercises, and Orchestral Excerpts

Moderato to Allegro
m.b., legato

4.

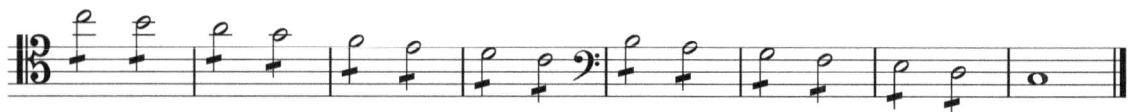

Slurred Bowings

The following routine, utilizing bowings 5–9, can also act as a basic warm-up that will get the blood flowing and the muscles toned.

Bowings 5–9 should be played with a similar approach to bowings 1–4. Increasing speed will be accomplished by each of these exercises having shorter note values than the one before. Concentrate on strict left-hand accuracy, much as a competent pianist uses in fingering rapid passages. Your fingers are the metronome in these exercises.

For daily practice, include 5, 6, 6a, and 7 (or 8 or 9). Your objectives here are similar to those for Sustained Bowings. Although various tempo versions are indicated, for 7, 8, and 9, start with a slower tempo and repeat a bowing several times, increasing speed with each playing. At least one version of either 7, 8, 9, 10, 11, or 11a should be included in practice of slurred bowings.

Perfecting Techniques through Employing Scales, Exercises, and Orchestral Excerpts

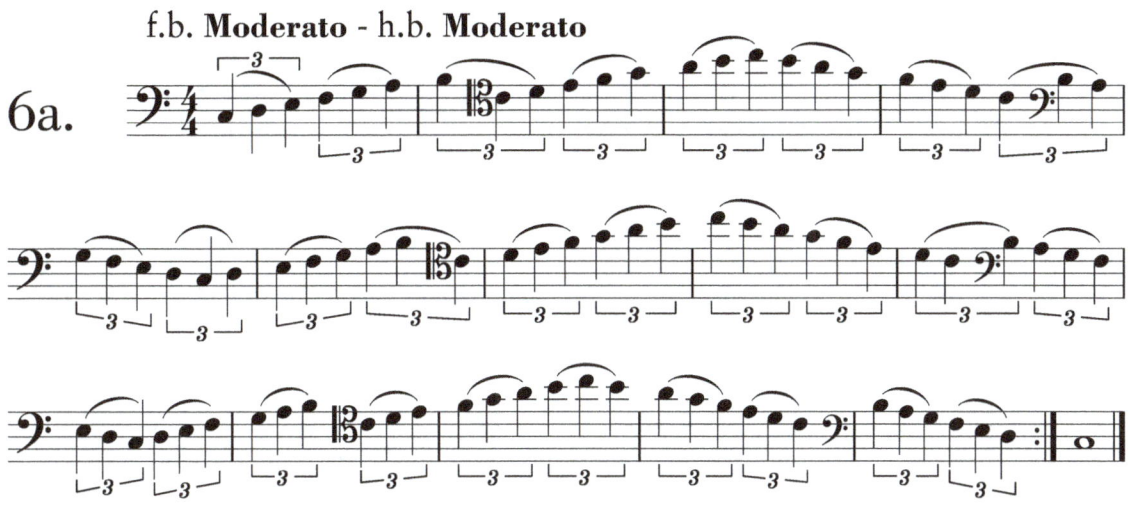

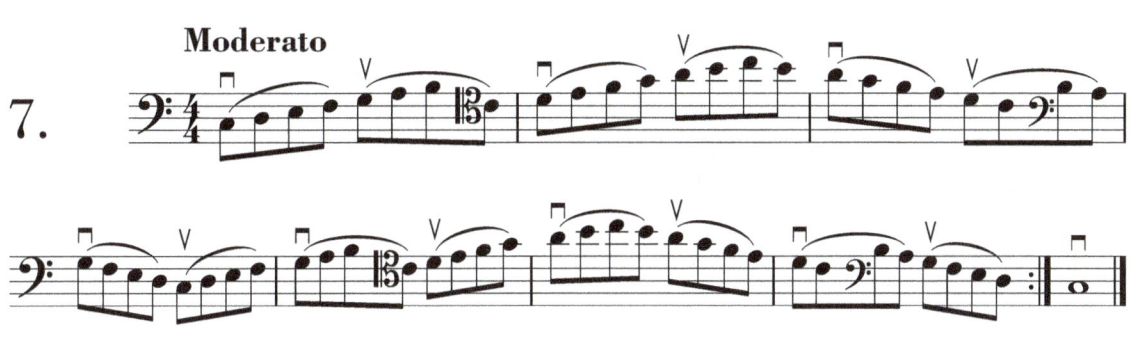

Perfecting Techniques through Employing Scales, Exercises, and Orchestral Excerpts

Andante - Allegro

9.

Slurring examples up to this point were typical through the nineteenth century. Around the twentieth century, more uneven patterns evolved, and now any combination of slurred bowings are present in solo, chamber, and orchestral compositions. Exercises 10 and 11 are examples of these more contemporary slurring patterns. In addition, combining multiple patterns (e.g., slur 2 + 3 + 4 or 4 + 2 + 3 or 1 + 2 + 2 etc.) should be experienced.

Andante - Allegro

10.

30

Perfecting Techniques through Employing Scales, Exercises, and Orchestral Excerpts

Maintain even quality and volume for bowings 11 and 11a. Do not surge on two slurred notes.

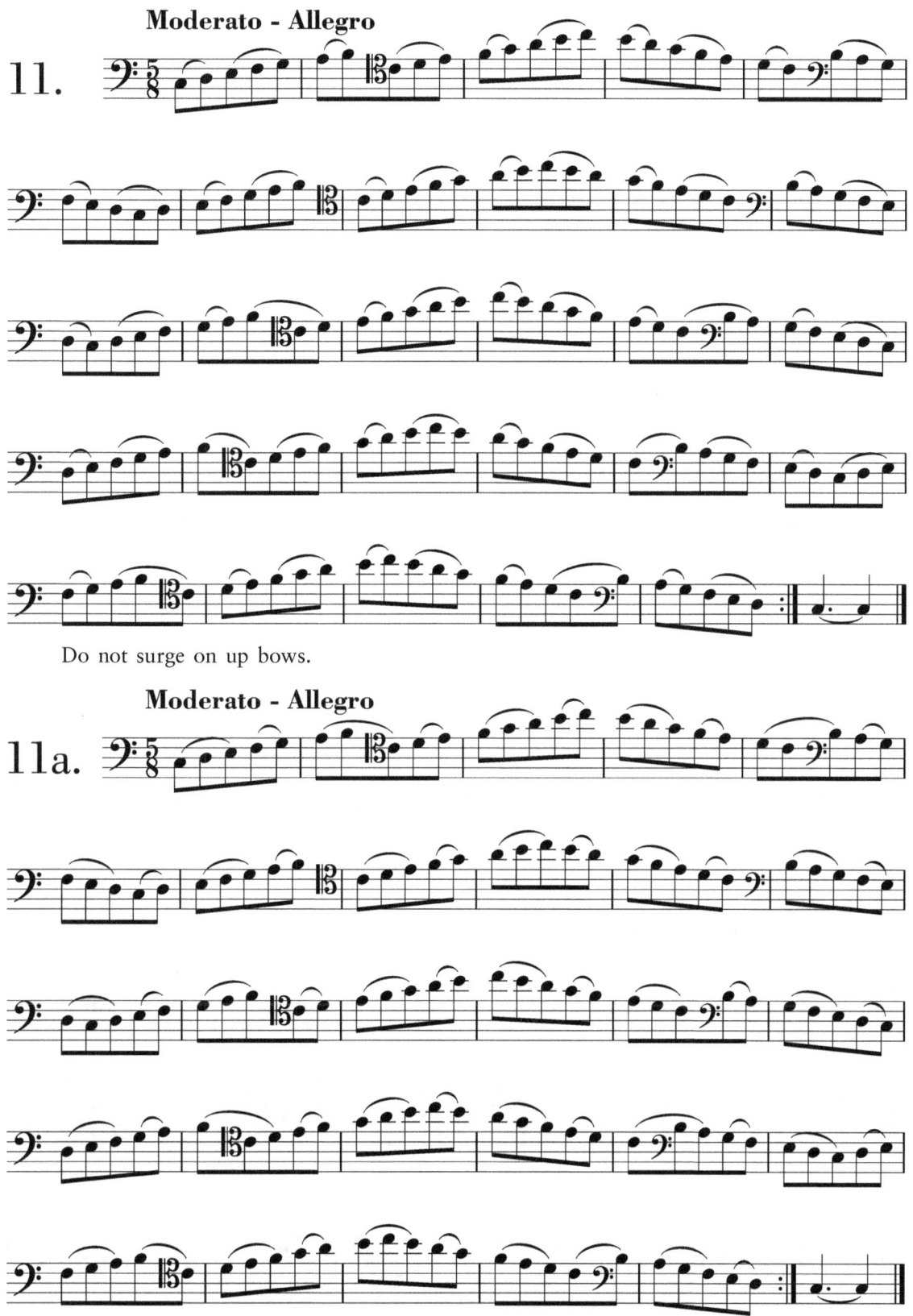

Do not surge on up bows.

Perfecting Techniques through Employing Scales, Exercises, and Orchestral Excerpts

Recovery Bowing

Exercises 12, 12a, and 12b are practice in recovery bowings. The objective should be a controlled replacement of the bow, at the same point of contact as the beginning of the previous stroke, recreating the same sound qualities (attack or legato, piano, or forte) and bow speed of the previous stroke.

- The objective is to achieve this bow recovery with the shortest rest between bow strokes.
- Use this same process starting strokes up-bow only.
- Play either with using attacks or legato, but maintain only one approach throughout one playing of the scale.
- Also play 12, 12a, and 12b using up-bow recovery.
- Now also alternate performing one bar forte and the next bar piano, etc. Maintain symmetry of tonal qualities in all registers.

Play using the smallest rest possible between strokes.

Perfecting Techniques through Employing Scales, Exercises, and Orchestral Excerpts

Alternating Patterns

(Daily include 13 or 14 plus 15, 16, and 17)

Exercises 13–17 are based on similar bowings. They can be played either legato or marcato/staccato. This pattern should be played in both versions. At slow tempo, legato is a normal expectation although a marcato/staccato version can also be required. Start slowly, increase tempo for each replay of the scale. At moderate tempos either legato or marcato/staccato is possible. At a fast tempo, a staccato articulation is most usual. However, practicing both articulations at different tempos will be beneficial for bow control.

For orchestral excerpts using versions of bowings 13–17, see Beethoven V,VI (p. 78–79), Mozart 40 (p. 92), Mozart 40, 41 (p. 92-93), Tchaikovsky, "Trepak," Romeo and Juliet (p. 99).

Practice examples 14 and 15 using instructions and bowings from example 13a and 13b.

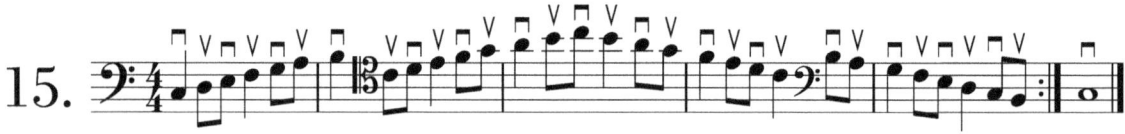

Note that the bowing illustrated in bowings 16 and 17 is the same pattern as used in the last movement of Mozart's Symphony no. 40 (p. 92). To execute this bowing in this Mozart passage, all bowing articulations should be enunciated (performed with a marcato-style stroke). The slur in this case binds two notes together but starts with a sharply defined (articulated) stroke.

For an orchestral excerpt using this bowing, see Mozart Symphony no. 40, IV (p. 92).

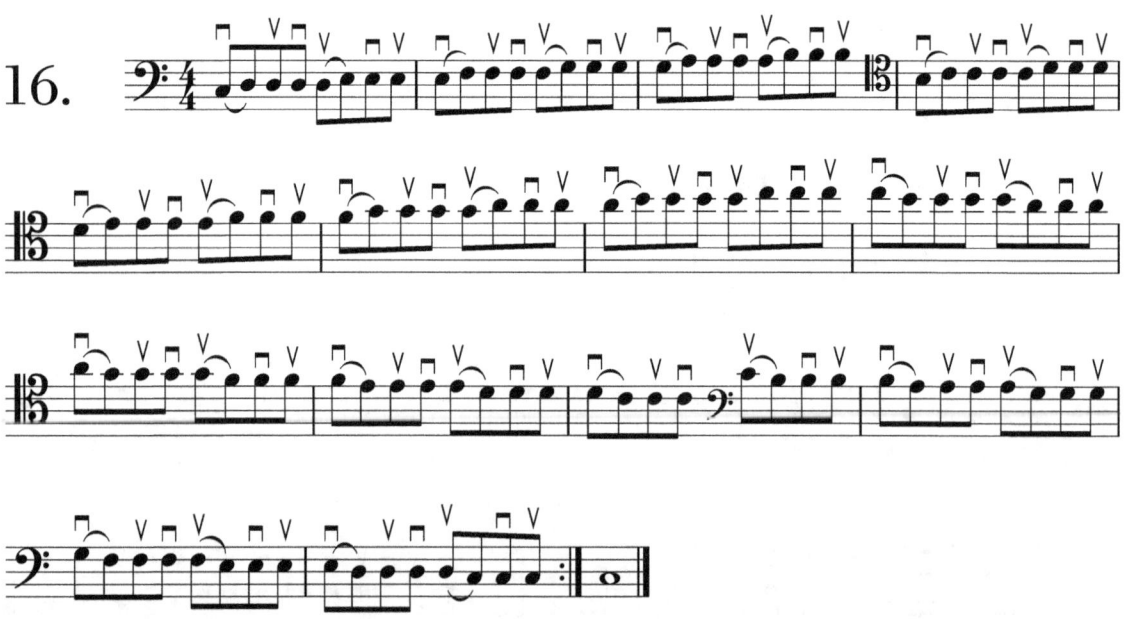

Perfecting Techniques through Employing Scales, Exercises, and Orchestral Excerpts

At faster tempos, use example 13b.

Staccato Bowing

Exercises 18–20b are to be used for staccato bowing practice. Staccato should sound short, deep, without scratching. In reality a staccato stroke starts with a bite (accent), whether it's forte or piano. The piano staccato is merely a very soft bite.

It doesn't matter whether a stroke is short or long, as there must always be follow-through. Follow-through is the additional controlled distance the arm/bow must travel in order to dissipate the thrust/energy created by the stroke. Not allowing follow-through requires a braking effort by the arm muscles; tending to choke the bow sound. This causes extra muscular tension/effort to stop the bow before the natural dissipation of the physical effort and the natural flow of motion. This can also result in undesirable tonal consequences.

Follow-through is part of almost all physical efforts. Think of the follow-through used in baseball by pitchers, batters, and all ball players throwing a ball. It is a means of allowing energy to more naturally dissipate rather than being choked off. It prevents unnecessary muscular effort and tension, allowing muscles and motion to come to a more comfortable and controllable stopping point.

Alternate daily, playing either 18, 19a, or 19b.

For an orchestral excerpt using this bowing, see Beethoven V, third movement, p. 78 (quarter notes).

Moderato - Allegro Vivace

Perfecting Techniques through Employing Scales, Exercises, and Orchestral Excerpts

Hooked Bowing

Bowing exercises 20 and 21 are for hooked-bowing practice. It is interesting to note that the slur and dot as written comprise a specific bowing marking used only for string instruments, but when written for any other family of musical instruments would indicate the elongation of the dotted quarter and shortening of the eighth note. For the string player it is also used as a bowing stroke that instructs one not to retake or change direction of the bow but continue in same direction with a marcato articulation of both note values.

When played quickly, as in the first movement of Schubert's Symphony no. 9, the articulation changes to the staccato/marcato character of the dotted eighth and sixteenth bowing used in exercises 22 and 23.

The articulation of the bowing in Exercises 22 and 23 is physically articulated differently than the markings on the page. The dotted eighth is not hooked to the following sixteenth, but rather is preceded by a reflex motion on the sixteenth immediately rebounding into the following dotted-eighth. It is the same reflex motion as one uses when playing a figure of two consecutive sixteenths in an Allegro tempo. It is an interdependent double motion that feels like a single effort with a rebound. Thus the bowing effort is sixteenth to dotted-eighth not as written and inferred by the tie/slur that dotted-eighth is hooked to the following sixteenth.

Practice this stroke slowly and "artificially" by performing a triple dotted quarter note followed by a sixty-fourth note going to the next double triple-dotted quarter note, etc. The objective is to practice the short note at a very fast speed, anticipating the reflex motion necessary, while elongating the quadruple-dotted quarter, providing time to intellectualize the direction and articulation of the reflex motion. As you achieve comfortable control of the reflex motion, you can increase your tempos and practice the bowing in a more realistic dotted-eighth sixteenth rhythmic relationship.

Alternate daily playing either 20 + 22 or 21 + 23.

Perfecting Techniques through Employing Scales, Exercises, and Orchestral Excerpts

For orchestral excerpts using this bowing, see Schubert IX, first movement, p. 95.

Perfecting Techniques through Employing Scales, Exercises, and Orchestral Excerpts

Spiccato Bowing

Exercises 24, 25, and 26 focus on the spiccato bowing. Spiccato has been described as a "bouncing bow" stroke, which is basically true. However, the bounce is a controlled and directed bounce. The height of the bounce and angle of the bow hair being thrust at the string must be very specific or the resultant sound will either be less centered (brushy) or too pinpointed and "picky" sounding.

The bounce for the spiccato should never be exaggerated by being too high or too wide. Too wide a bounce results in a brushier contact with string. Bouncing too high results in less ability for control of both sound production and metronomic accuracy. Proper thrust, height, and width of stroke will control the success of the spiccato. Use no more or less motion than required to achieve the thrust that provides a clean, resonant bite at the vortex of the spiccato. A good spiccato will sound clean and deep and have a round "ping" like a pizzicato.

It is possible to lack control of the spiccato if either bounce is too high or low, of if the width of the stroke is too wide or narrow (the angle of thrust toward the string is too wide or too narrow). Spiccato, even in pianissimo, is an aggressive stroke and must have a properly integrated motion to create positive results. It is a bowing in which the fingers of the bow arm have a more important and active role to play than in most other bowings.

The very rapid spiccato or sautillé will require a moderate bending and unbending motion at the elbow hinge, very much like a pumping motion. The arm can move rapidly in this manner, much as it does in a tremolo, and will not become stiff, as it does when trying to play very rapid strokes with a locked elbow joint. This manner of use for the elbow joint relates only to very fast (shorter) bow strokes and not longer, sustained bowings.

Finally, each speed and volume will have some effect on the shaping that is required to create a proper-sounding spiccato. The faster the stroke, the more motion decreases. The bounce will be less visible, as will the back and forth movement of the bow.

For orchestral excerpts using this stroke, see Beethoven I and III (p. 77), Mozart 39, 40, and 41 (p. 90–94).

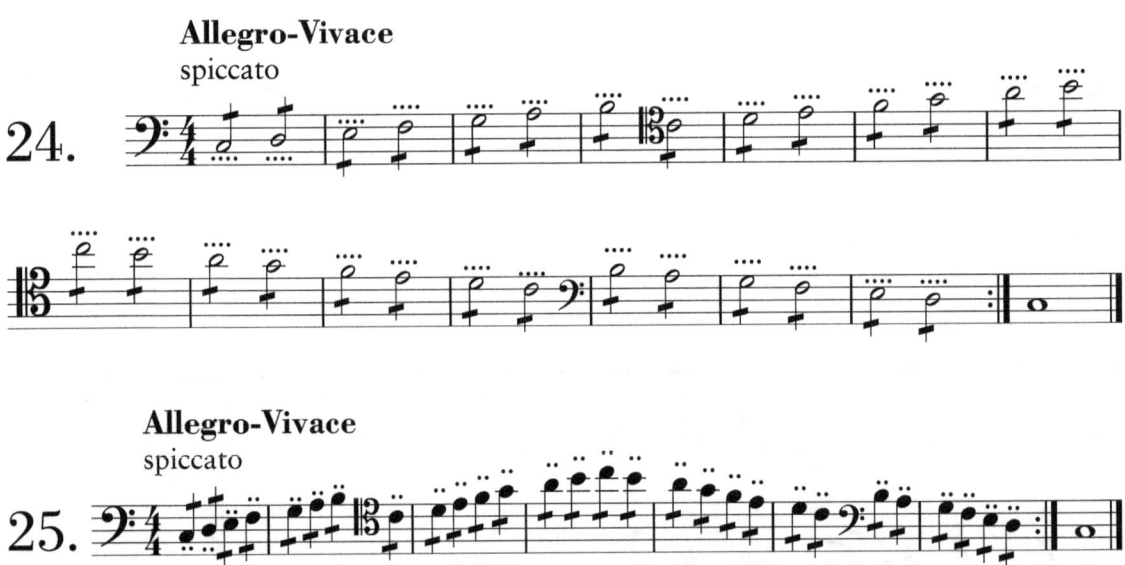

Perfecting Techniques through Employing Scales, Exercises, and Orchestral Excerpts

Allegro-Vivace
spiccato

26.

Spiccato should also be played five strokes per pitch and alternating combinations of (2+3) (3+2) (3 + 4) (4 + 3) (1 + 2 + 3) etc.

Bow Recovery

Exercises 27 and 28 deal with bow recovery. In Exercise 27, you should bring your bow back toward the frog of the bow and place it firmly on the string before playing the pick-up eighth-note. Not doing so causes one to exaggerate the articulation of the eighth note, in the anxiety of rushing back to the frog to cover the exaggerated distance in order to play the next dotted-quarter at the frog.

This process of retrieval, or recovery, is required in many figures where elongated notation leaves one at the tip end of the bow, when a preparatory short up-bow is required for the next portion of a passage or rhythm. The act of bow recovery should occur before the short note. As stated, neglect in using the practice of retrieval or bow recovery before playing shorter pick-up note will usually result in an unintended surge and exaggeration of the short stroke when articulated before recovery.

This bowing has tempo/speed limitations. When played in fast Allegro, it is usually played as a hooked bowing:

R = retrieve/recover.

Bowings 29, 30, 31, and 32 are used in slow and fast tempos. In slow tempos, two simple up-bow staccatos fulfill the obligations of the stroke. In fast tempos, the articulation is more complex and more challenging to control. Now, two up-bow spiccatos are required that are perfectly placed rhythmically and tonally. Here you should be controlling the same bowing elements (techniques) as described under spiccato bowing.

You will find it more challenging to play two controlled spiccato strokes in one direction. As before, do not bounce any higher than necessary, and angle your bow

Perfecting Techniques through Employing Scales, Exercises, and Orchestral Excerpts

direction to achieve clarity of pitch and articulation. You will find this stroke will require the up-bows to lean toward using a somewhat stingy length of bow. Carefully direct the thrust of the up-bow, do not just throw it loosely.

In a slower tempo that requires the bouncing up-bow, you may need to retrieve some bow length and place the up-bow spiccatos closer toward the frog. This will provide a more centered up-bow spiccato and more bow control.

For orchestral excerpts using this bowing, see Mozart 41, first movement, p. 93.

Perfecting Techniques through Employing Scales, Exercises, and Orchestral Excerpts

32.

Bowings 33–36 are most important in that they are such a perfect examples of how misleading markings on the printed page can be as related to actual bowing motions (maneuvers) required. As previously described for the dotted-eighth and sixteenth stroke, the sixteenth recoils into the dotted-eighth in one reflex motion. It is the same for bowings in 33–39. Most significant, however, is that physically the bowing really starts with the sixteenth note hooked into the eighth, recoiling back to the placement for the coming dotted-eighth. In essence the bowing is

this: ♫ | ♪ not this: ♩. ♫

The tie mark on the printed page above the dotted-eighth and sixteenth erroneously leads one to envisioning a different physical pattern. Even as Beethoven wrote the theme, this rhythm actually is:

♫ | ♩. ♫ | ♩. ♪ ♫ | ♩. ♫ ♩. ♫ | etc.

For orchestral excerpts using bowing examples 33–36, see Beethoven VII, first movement (p. 80).

Moderato - Allegro Vivace

33.

34.

42

Perfecting Techniques through Employing Scales, Exercises, and Orchestral Excerpts

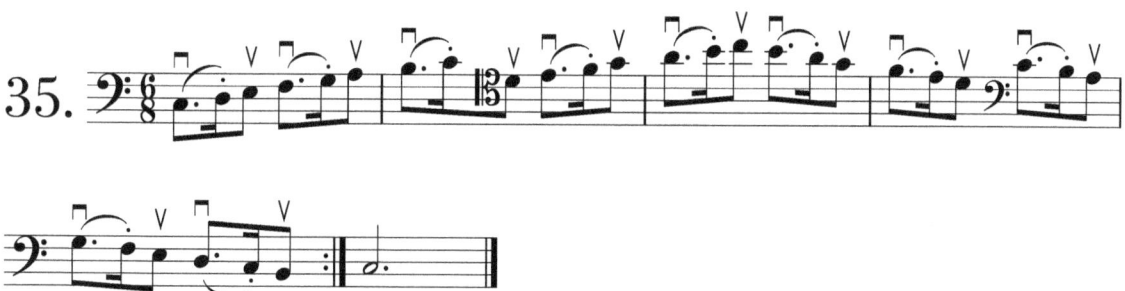

Similar articulation in reverse. Bowing stroke starts on ♪ → ♪ ♪ | ♪ ♩.

Exercise 37 is included to emphasize that playing slurs across beats or pulses should not result in the second note of the slur receiving any bowing emphasis. It should sound the same as a slurred bowing that starts on the beat. It should not sound syncopated. Make sure the slurring of the second note is a pure legato into the next note and does not cause any audible stressing of the second note of the slur.

Andante - Vivace
Syncopated bowing

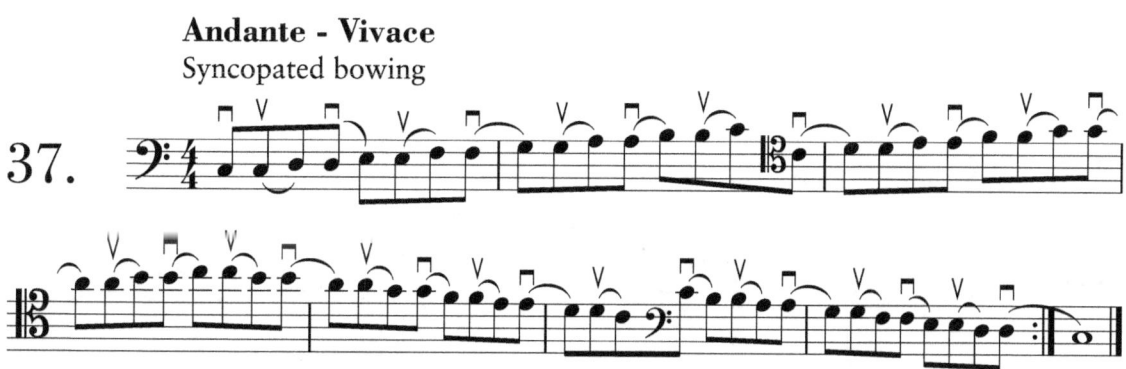

Perfecting Techniques through Employing Scales, Exercises, and Orchestral Excerpts

Recovery patterns

Bowings 38–40 pose the question: Do we use bow recovery before or after the short pick-up note? Tempo mostly determines this. In slower or moderate tempos, it is feasible to recover before the separate eighth note. This is done to avoid the unintended accenting of the up-bow in the anxiety of getting back toward the frog for the down-bow. In fast tempos, whether recovering before or after the short stroke, the up-bow (short stroke) should be no louder or more accented than the longer stroke. If possible, using recovery could avoid this problem, but when it is too rapid a tempo for that, it is possible to lighten the up-bow motion by trying to play it before the up-bow thrust for recovery. Practice the stroke slowly and try and psych yourself into having the sensation of playing the up-bow note a split second before the thrust of the up-bow occurs. Then, of course, speed up the effort until you can achieve control over the thrust of the up-bow, so that it doesn't cause a sound explosion that overshadows the down-bow. If successful, you should feel the sensation of the up-bow being part of the continued pressure or the preceding down-bow (after which the actual up-bow motion starts for the return toward the frog, in preparation for the next down-bow).

Proper execution of these bowings is very demanding, and is very often unsuccessfully done. It will take a lot of work and analytical concentration to be successful in avoiding the surging accented up-bow (a very unfortunate, unconscious habit that often occurs in string playing).

For an orchestral excerpt using this bowing, see Berlioz: Roman Carnival Overture (p. 84).

Perfecting Techniques through Employing Scales, Exercises, and Orchestral Excerpts

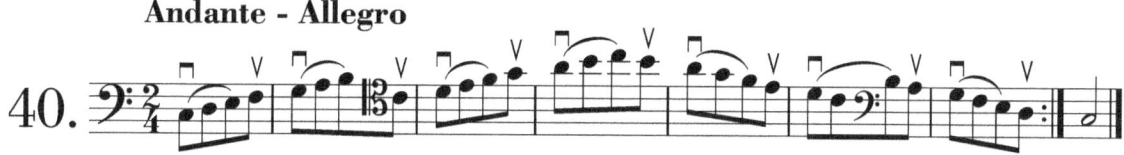

Reverse Recovery Bowings

Bowings 41–43 are the reverse challenge to the preceding bowing group. Here we have to avoid the exaggerated accent of the down-bow usually followed by an up-bow lacking equal volume.

Playing very slowly, try starting the pattern in Exercise 42 on the slurred up-bow notes. Play them with a moderate attack and then follow them with a short down-bow with less volume and attack. Try skipping after the down-bow (short stroke) to the bow placement needed for a comfortable up-bow (containing two slurred notes). Do this very artificially, ending with the down-bow sounding softer than the up-bow. Slowly increase the speed of this effort, maintaining a louder up-bow. You will find it takes just a peck or touch of the bow on the down-bow and then a firmer placement of the bow for the up-bow. After doing this in several tempos that are within your control, realize that it is after all possible to play the down-bow without exaggeration as compared to the up-bow.

Now work to balance out the volume and articulation of the up- and down-bows so that they sound more equal musically and not exaggerated. Achieving the desired result is another example of mind over matter.

Perfecting Techniques through Employing Scales, Exercises, and Orchestral Excerpts

Bowings 44 and 45 are again a recovery-type bowing. Always bring the up-bow back toward the frog before executing the down-bow.

More "Bouncing" Bow Strokes

As already indicated, bowing 46 and 47, when played in moderate tempos, would be played spiccato. At faster tempos the bowing may become a sautillé. In the slower off-the-string bowing (spiccato), the elbow generally remains in its usual shaping and does not become a moving hinge. In going to the really fast spiccato or sautillé, the elbow joint becomes an active hinge. The arm now takes on more of a moderate pumping action, rather than just moving back and forth as a solid unit. The sautillé motion is akin to the tremolo, where one should be using the elbow hinge in a pumping motion. In a spiccato, we want the bow to bounce rhythmically, while in a tremolo, we press the bow more into the string to prevent a bounce and create a rubbing action rather than a ricochet or bouncing action. There is no attempt at a rhythmic result implied in a tremolo, but most of us usually move in a regular speed when playing tremolo. This, of course, is actually playing in one speed or rhythm, but with each member of a section hopefully playing tremolo at a different speed, the result is an intense sounding non-rhythmic rumble.

Exercises 46 and 47 near balance of bow. Fast spiccato (sautillé).

Syncopated Bowings

When playing Bowings 48 and 49, the objective is to achieve a pure slur without any unconscious surging into the second slurred note caused by syncopated slurring. Play as smoothly and connected as possible. The habit of unconsciously accenting syncopated notes within a slur is widespread and musically distorting.

Perfecting Techniques through Employing Scales, Exercises, and Orchestral Excerpts

Hooked Staccato Stroke

Bowings 50 and 51 are staccato exercises created by causing very short bowing impulses. Physically, they are very similar to the physical process used for making attacks, but are a series of successive attacks or impulses in one direction, rather than the usual rotation of up- and down-bows.

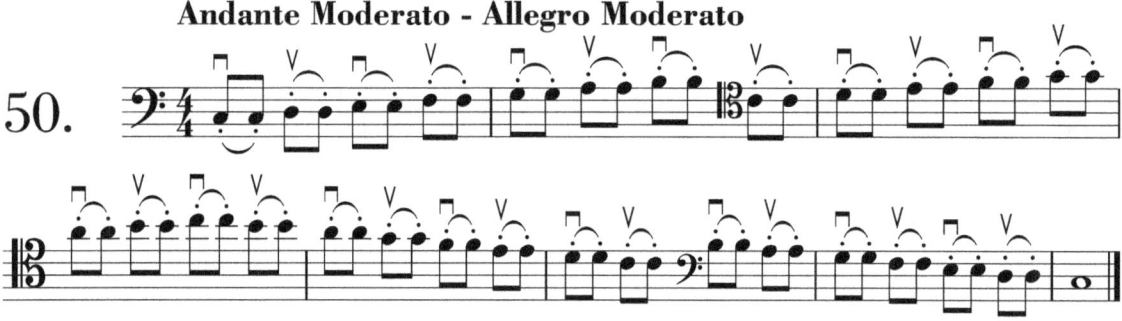

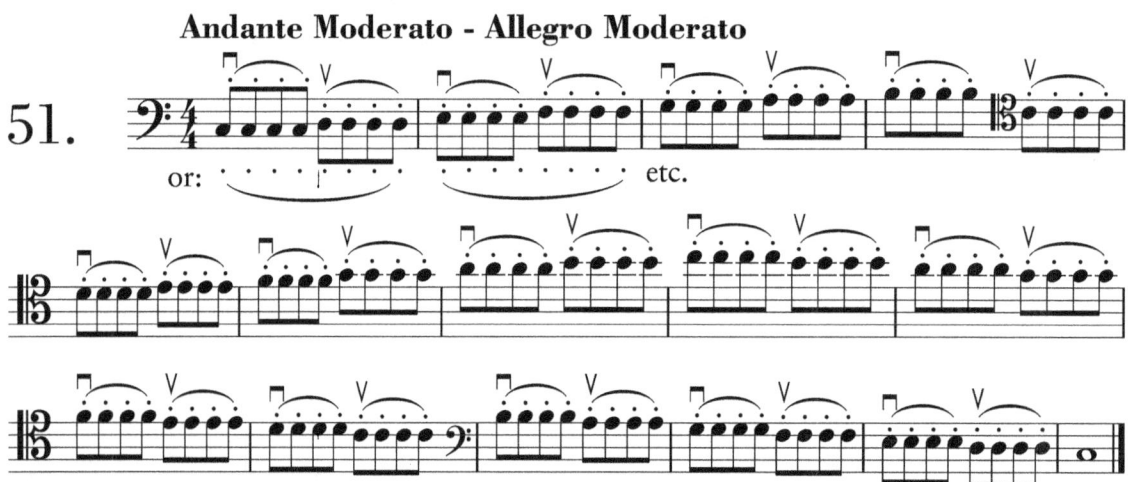

Perfecting Techniques through Employing Scales, Exercises, and Orchestral Excerpts

"Reflex" Bowings

Bowings 52 and 53 should be performed in lower part of the bow for forte passages and somewhere around the middle or slightly past the middle of the bow for piano nuances. These bowings are more often found in orchestral passages rather than in study books or solo works. The resultant bowing at allegro tempos, will sound like two short (staccato) notes of the same length rather than what is written on the page. Practice these bowings in piano and forte. Although seemingly different visually, the physical motion is the same as playing two sixteenth notes in a rapid tempo, with the first sixteenth on the beat (or with first sixteenth preceding the beat).

The stroke is another reflex motion like the playing of two rapid sixteenth or thirty-second notes in succession.

For orchestral excerpts using this bowing, see Berlioz: Symphonie Fantastique, fourth movement (p. 84-85).

Conclusion

The bowings that should be included in daily practice are in examples 1–11a, 13–17, 20–23, and 24–26. The bowings not included above can be alternated by including one or more of them in your daily routine. For daily bowing practice, use only one major or minor scale per day, include arpeggios and chromatic scale based on same tonality.

Perfecting Techniques through Employing Scales, Exercises, and Orchestral Excerpts

Bowing Etudes

These exercises are deliberately created to be uncomplicated and undemanding for the left hand, in order to allow total concentration on performing the bowing strokes to be used with these exercises. Choose bowing patterns from the previous fifty-three examples presented in Section IIA. You will note that the following exercises in duple and triple meters allow the use of duplet or triplet bowings with appropriate exercise.

Use moderate tempos for initial practice of exercises with bowing patterns. Gradually increase tempos with each repeat of an exercise, until an exercise becomes challenging. Always keep working toward the next goal by trying to perfect the next faster tempo.

2 and 3-Octave Scales

Major - 2 Octave

A = Alternate Fingering
W = Without open strings
E = Extending thumb position
M = Most maneuverable fingering

Perfecting Techniques through Employing Scales, Exercises, and Orchestral Excerpts

Perfecting Techniques through Employing Scales, Exercises, and Orchestral Excerpts

Major - 3 Octave

Perfecting Techniques through Employing Scales, Exercises, and Orchestral Excerpts

Perfecting Techniques through Employing Scales, Exercises, and Orchestral Excerpts

Melodic Minor Scales

Note that, for major scales, multiple fingering possibilities were provided. For minor scales, some alternative fingering options are given. At this point, it is now your challenge to find other possible fingerings for minor scales employing use of the thumb when reasonable and beneficial.

Perfecting Techniques through Employing Scales, Exercises, and Orchestral Excerpts

Perfecting Techniques through Employing Scales, Exercises, and Orchestral Excerpts

Perfecting Techniques through Employing Scales, Exercises, and Orchestral Excerpts

Harmonic Minor Scales

In pre-thumb position, harmonic minor scales allow for an interesting fingering between the 5th, flat-6th and 7th degrees of the scale. When a scale allows the 7th to be played on the G string, it is possible to arrange fingering so that the 5th and flat 6th are fingered with 2nd and 4th fingers on D string, allowing the 7th to be directly across on the G string, using the 1st finger. You now have the option of playing the tonic with 2nd finger in same position or shifting a half step and playing tonic with 1st finger. The choice you make here should allow you to end up with the 4th finger on an f or f# preceding the shift into thumb position.

This fingering is only feasible for harmonic minor scales of A through E. It provides a smoother process for dealing with the augmented 2nd, between the 6th and 7th steps of harmonic minor scales.

Perfecting Techniques through Employing Scales, Exercises, and Orchestral Excerpts

Perfecting Techniques through Employing Scales, Exercises, and Orchestral Excerpts

Perfecting Techniques through Employing Scales, Exercises, and Orchestral Excerpts

2- and 3-Octave Arpeggio Fingerings

The practice of arpeggios is essential to the shifting process for larger intervals, as scales are for developing mobility and accuracy in diatonic passages. It is another area of finite mobility essential to tactile memory.

Always start practicing arpeggios slowly, concentrating on preparation and balance for a comfortable shift. Shift with minimal required pressure using the string as a track. Make most of the shifting motion on the same string as the pitch that is your goal. Do not continue to the next required shift unless accuracy has been achieved on the current shift. Your goals are a relaxed, smooth shift; accuracy of pitch and proper timing to arrive at next pulse (beat).

Do not continue shifting to the next pitch of an arpeggio unless you have achieved pitch accuracy with the current shift. Keep in mind that it is the arm that shifts the hand, allowing it to glide to the next pitch, before putting on the brakes (pressure to secure a new pitch).

When shifting is improved, include slurring two notes per bow on arpeggios. You will now be able to judge more critically how cleanly you are shifting. When shifting is comfortable and predictable, practice slurring groups of three and finally groups of four. Note that the printed arpeggios below do not repeat tonics. Use this approach for arpeggio practice, as it encourages more shifting accuracy. Practice one arpeggio each day based on the tonic chord of the scale used for that day's practice.

2-Octave Arpeggio Fingerings

Perfecting Techniques through Employing Scales, Exercises, and Orchestral Excerpts

3-Octave Arpeggio Fingerings

Andante - Allegro

Chromatic Scales

The practice and perfection of chromatic scales is one of the most important efforts we can make to improve intonation and learn fingering patterns that are unique to chromatic passages. We all recognize that the structure of the hand does not automatically create two equal half steps (between 1st and 2nd fingers or between 2nd and 4th fingers). Although this is information we believe that we have compensated for in order to maintain accurate intonation, try the following test: play a 2-octave F# chromatic scale and along the way, check your fingered D on the G string with the open D. Is it perfectly in tune? Similarly, check other intervals with an open string to insure that intonation is really accurate. Chromatic scales are a different aural experience than major or minor scales, and if you can play them with positive intonation, it will allow the perfecting of chromatic and diatonic passages and improve left-hand dexterity.

Like the other techniques discussed, my objective is organization of the intellectual process. The half-position, or initial position on a string, is usually the transitional position that sets up the fingering for the rest of a scale or scale-like passage. Our fingering objective (in chromatic scales) once we leave half-position on the G string is to have a constant pattern of fingering 1, 2, 4 until we reach the highest tonic in pre-thumb position (or 1, 2, 3) in thumb position for chromatic scales). For scales that do not go into thumb position, the fingering in half-position on the G string will either be 1st finger and shift, 1, 2 and shift, or 1, 2, 4 and shift.

A transitional position (or transitional fingering) is used to set up a constant fingering for the remainder of a passage. This position may also be referred to as the pivotal position or pivotal fingering. For chromatic scales, the transitional position will be half-position on the G string. In most cases, you will also find passages, whether they are chromatic, diatonic, or arpeggiated, that will have a transition point or position that sets up fingering for the rest of the passage. For diatonic scales for instance, the fingering in the lowest position used on a string should allow the remainder of the passage to be fingered 1, 4 or 2, 4, until ending the ascending passage with the 4th finger. The descending version of the same passage will employ the same fingering used for the ascending portion of the passage, but in reverse. As is usually the case, rules may have exceptions, but are essential basic guides that are most often applicable.

In pre-thumb position chromatic scales, the transitional position will be half-position, allowing for all following positions to play out the hand (fingering: 1, 2, 4 in ascending patterns or 4, 2, 1 in descending scales). Establishing and memorizing fixed fingering practices will create automatic responses, essential for sight-reading.

As stated, almost all extended stepwise passages, whether diatonic or chromatic, require a transition position. This is usually the lowest required position on a string. As already stated, the fingering chosen for that position should set up playing out the hand. Thus, diatonically, if you have a five-note (step-wise) ascending figure to be played on one string, one note will be played in the lowest transition position while the other notes are paired in twos for all following positions. If you have an odd-numbered series of notes on one string moving diatonically in one direction, then one note will be played in the lowest position and the other notes will be paired in following position(s), using fingering 1, 4 or 2, 4 (depending on the interval required). It is likely; you have been using these practices but may not have recognized them as logical rules of fingering. If the passage contains an even number of notes moving diatonically in one direction, the pivotal position, as well as the remainder of the passage, would be fingered using two notes per position.

The system is similar for chromatic scales that go into thumb position. The most practical fingering leading to thumb position is to follow 4th-finger F# with thumb on the octave G (on the G string). For chromatic scales going into thumb position, we have a constant fingering on the G string . We are always going to set up the preceding F# with a 4th finger. Pre-thumb position fingering on the G string will now will require using 2nd finger on A in half position, then shifting and playing 1, 2, 4 up through the F# preceding thumb position.

The transitional thumb position will now be composed of the first 3-fingered notes (G#, A and B-flat, fingered 1, 2, 3), which coincidentally are the same three pitch names as in half-position on the G string. Therefore, the process for determining the transitional fingering for the first three notes in thumb position will require using a system similar to what we will use in pre-thumb position.

I now offer a system to help remember fingering for chromatic scales. The explanation may seem cumbersome, but once intellectualized it is a functional easily managed process. As already stated, the pivotal fingering in half position on the G-string is determined by the successive number of fingered notes required to complete the scale. For chromatic scales not going into thumb position, the pivotal half-position fingerings are G# (1) and shift, or A (1, 2) and shift, or A# (1, 2, 4) and shift. The scales that require only G# (1) in half-position to set up remaining scale fingering are G#, B, D, F. How can you remember that? If you examine these scale names, you will find they coincidentally form a fully diminished seventh chord. In other words, if you are asked to play an F-chromatic scale, spell the diminished seventh chord built on F until you name the pivot pitch in half position on the G string contained in that chord. By spelling F, A-flat, B, D-flat, you find the G string half-position note, Ab, which is also your pivot note for the B-chromatic scale. You need only spell the full diminished seventh chord until it names the half-position pivotal pitch (on G string) that becomes the pitch, after which you shift and then continue playing 1, 2, 4 until you reach the next tonic. If an F# chromatic scale is required, spell from F# and you find the next note in the dim. 7th chord is A, the half-position pivot note after which you will shift to set up the F# chromatic scale fingering. Any scale in a grouping of minor thirds uses the same pivotal pitch in half position on the G-string. There are only three cycles (groupings) of minor thirds, B, D, F, A-flat; C, E-flat, G-flat, B-double flat (A) and C#, E, G, B-flat. You only need spelling as much of a chord cycle as it takes to identify the pivot pitch in half-position on the G string. The process is really quite simple, once intellectually absorbed. You will even begin to instinctively remember the pivot note without the above process, after you have worked with chromatic scales for a time.

Perfecting Techniques through Employing Scales, Exercises, and Orchestral Excerpts

2-Octave Chromatic Scales

Fully dim. 7th chord

Perfecting Techniques through Employing Scales, Exercises, and Orchestral Excerpts

Fully dim. 7th chord

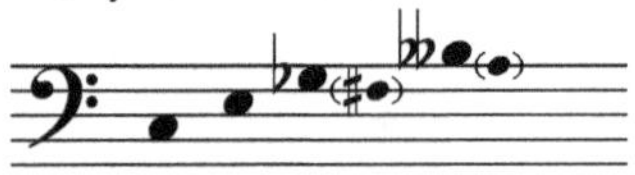

Perfecting Techniques through Employing Scales, Exercises, and Orchestral Excerpts

Fully dim. 7th chord

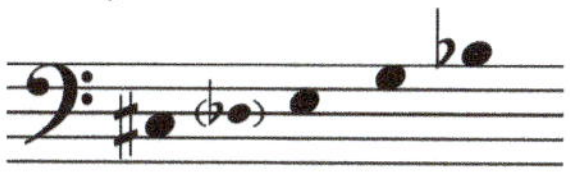

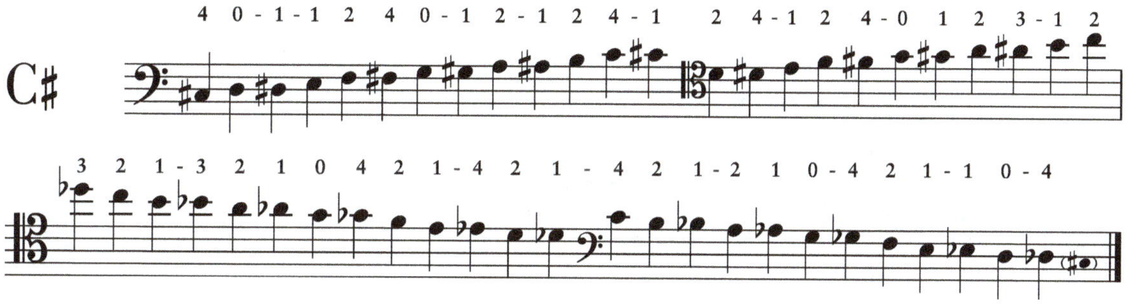

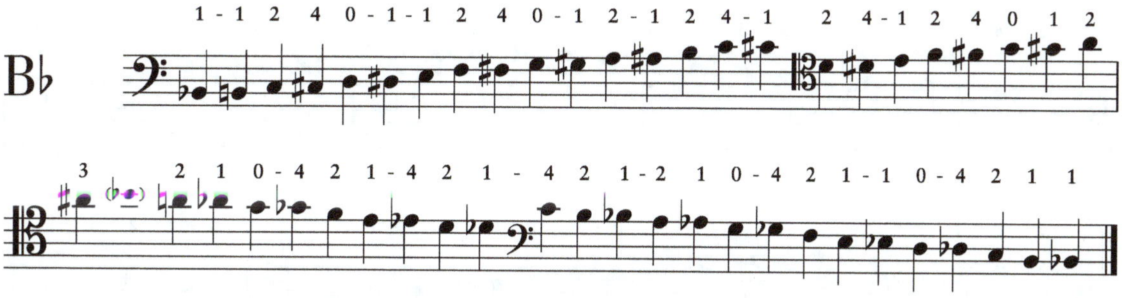

Perfecting Techniques through Employing Scales, Exercises, and Orchestral Excerpts

3-Octave Chromatic Scales

Perfecting Techniques through Employing Scales, Exercises, and Orchestral Excerpts

Perfecting Techniques through Employing Scales, Exercises, and Orchestral Excerpts

String Crossing Exercises

String crossings should be played using a minimal string-crossing motion that still allows for physical comfort. The bigger the motion, the more wasted effort and the more difficult the process of playing across strings becomes. On the other hand, we need to retain enough of this arcing pattern to retain rhythmic symmetry, as the body requires a certain minimal standard of movement, before it loses its measuring ability and resultant loss of control. Start with slower tempos that allow studying and refining your motion. Follow this by pursuing faster tempos that you can still control, and then find a faster tempo that challenges you. This faster tempo should be just a bit beyond the fastest tempo you are comfortable controlling.

These string-crossing patterns should be combined once you have achieved reasonable comfort and control of the basic string-crossing patterns. Combining means taking half a bar of one pattern and half a bar of another pattern, thus creating another exercise.

These patterns can also be practiced in scales as shown in exercises A, B, and C on the following page. You will additionally note that string crossing exercises are also presented in triplets.

All of the following examples can be started up bow or down bow and should be practiced both ways. The following string crossings are to be played without the use of open strings. Any two notes on adjacent strings can be employed.

(The G is always stopped with the 1st finger in the following exercises.)

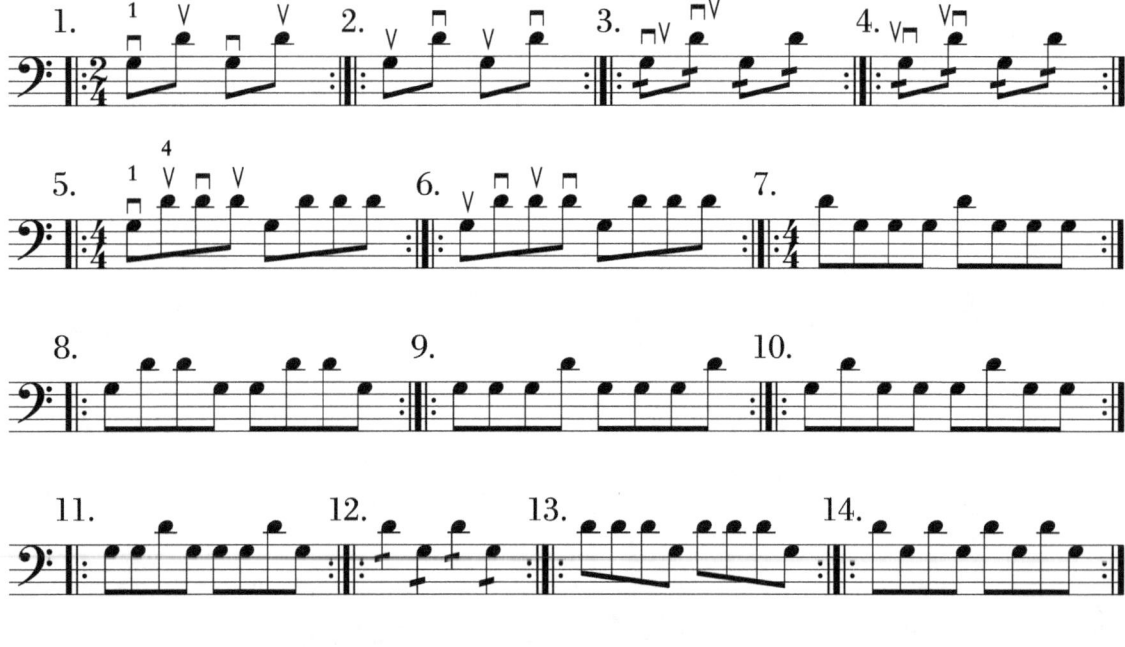

70

Perfecting Techniques through Employing Scales, Exercises, and Orchestral Excerpts

Below are examples of bowings as they can be practiced across strings using open D-string.

Most bowing exercises through 53 can be applied to string-crossing exercises.

Perfecting Techniques through Employing Scales, Exercises, and Orchestral Excerpts

Trill, Finger, and Shifting Exercises

In this section, the first four exercises are finger exercises that are excellent for warm-ups and developing stronger finger rhythm. Exercises 5–8 are either shifting or progressive fingering exercises. Accuracy, rhythmic fingering, and smoothness of shifting are the main focus. These exercises help develop facility and tactile identity of the fingerboard.

Play this rhythmic pattern with all finger combinations in different adjoining positions daily. For half-step fingering, the notation will of course be A# and B, or an equivalent depending on string position being used.

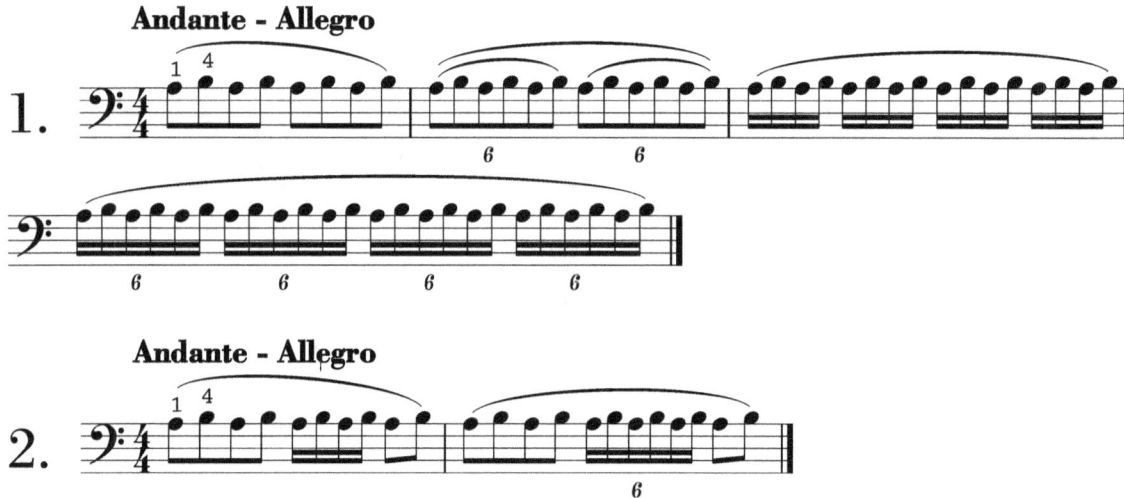

Practice in three adjoining positions, progressing up or down chromatically.

Play four times each in three adjoining higher positions.

Play exercises 5–8 in all keys in 1, 2, or 3 octaves.

Perfecting Techniques through Employing Scales, Exercises, and Orchestral Excerpts

Use this example in all keys.

6.

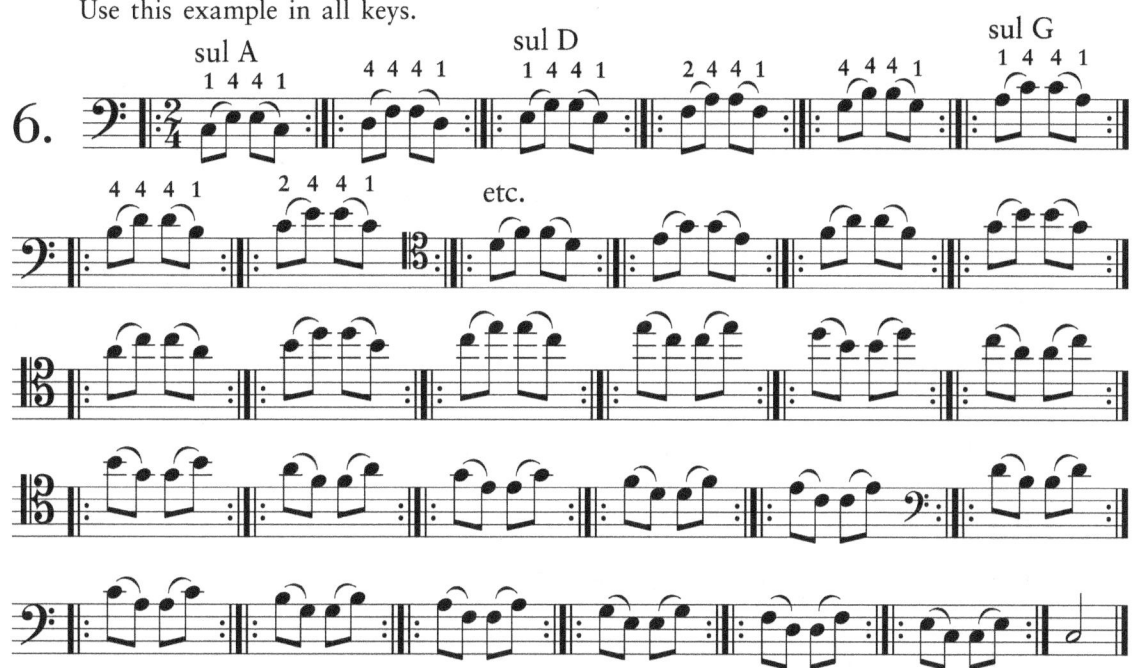

Play in all keys in 2- or 3-octave patterns, utilizing one key each day based on tonic of scale used for bowings that day. (2x) = Play the alternate fingering on the 2nd time through.

7.

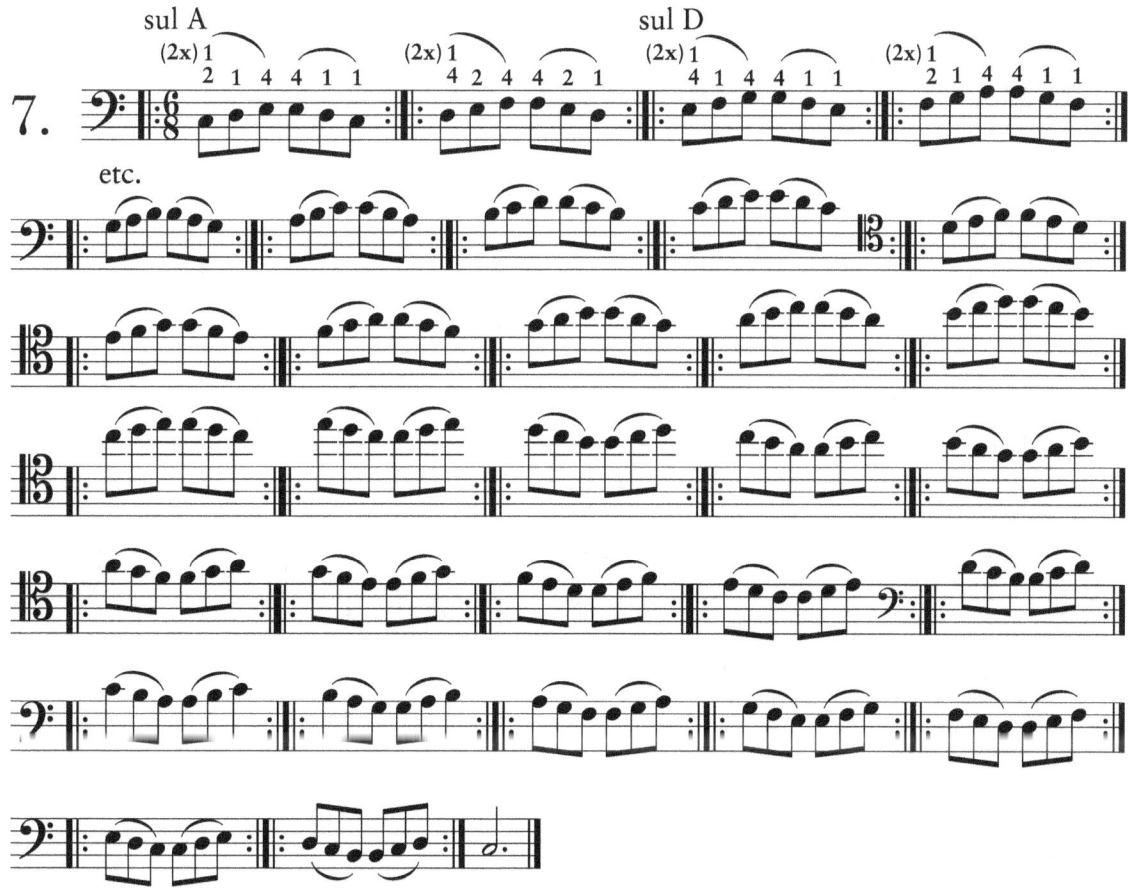

Perfecting Techniques through Employing Scales, Exercises, and Orchestral Excerpts

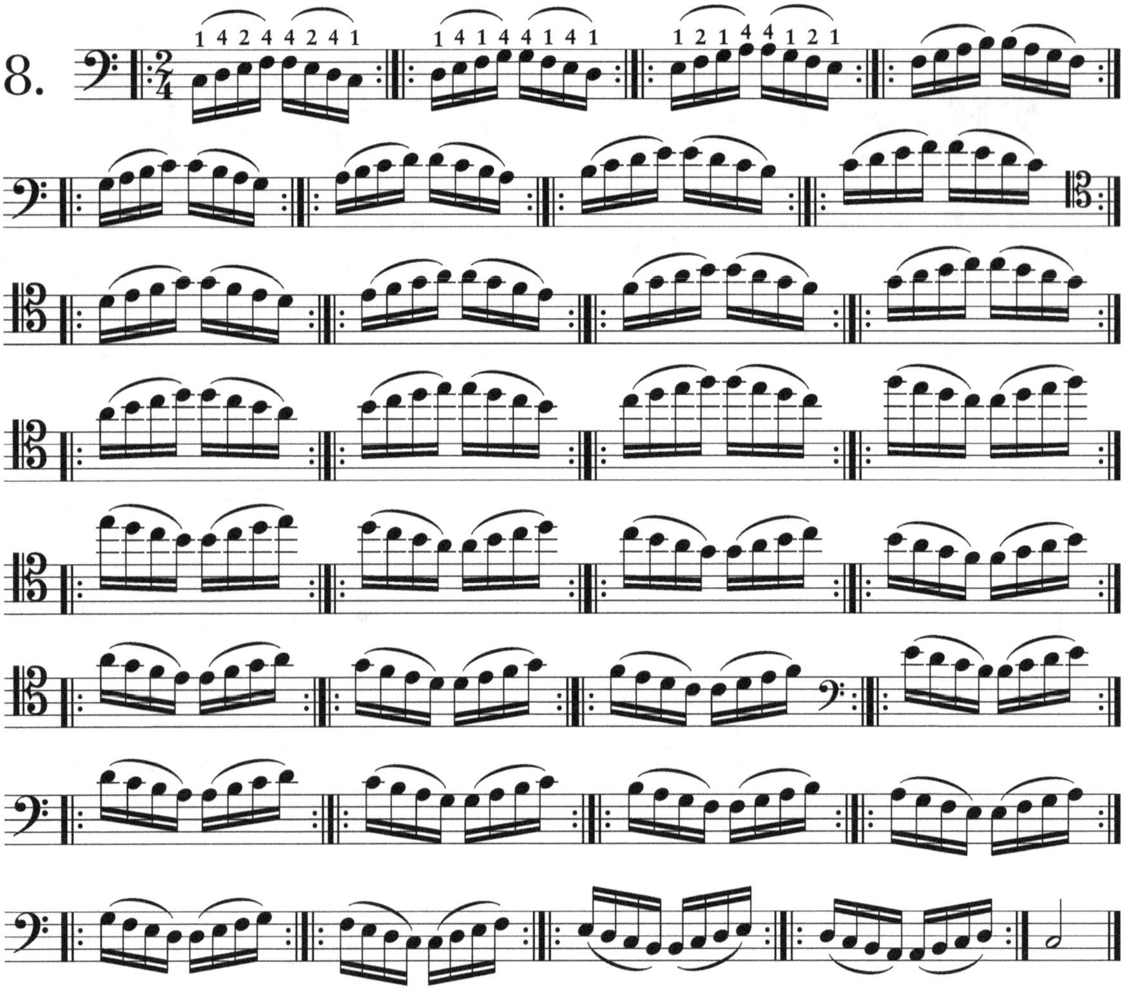

Play the following shifting examples in different keys (on one string). Many variations are possible.

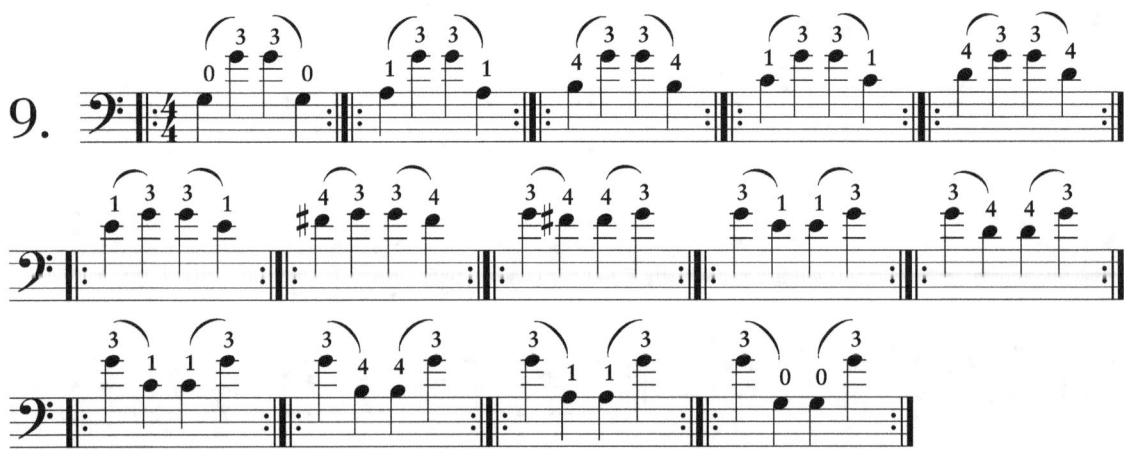

Perfecting Techniques through Employing Scales, Exercises, and Orchestral Excerpts

9 contd.

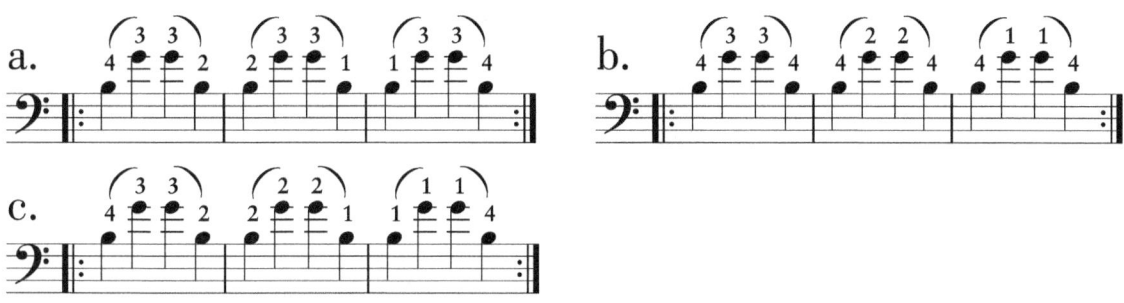

Introduction to Fingering
Across Strings in Thumb Position

Play everything in thumb position and across strings only. In some cases, notes indicated to be played with the 2nd finger may be played with the 3rd finger.

For an extensive exploration of fingering possibilities, see An Organized Method of String Playing by Murray Grodner. 47 pages. Published by Peer International.

Perfecting Techniques through Employing Scales, Exercises, and Orchestral Excerpts

Left-Hand Patterns for Shifting Dexterity

Play each exercise slowly until fingering is comfortable and instinctive. Increase tempo and master each speed before increasing speed. The goal should be eventually playing comfortably at a moderate allegro tempo. These exercises should also be practiced slurring 2 or 4 notes per bowing stroke.

To be played in all keys.

These examples can be expanded by playing groupings of six, seven, or eight.

To be played in all keys.

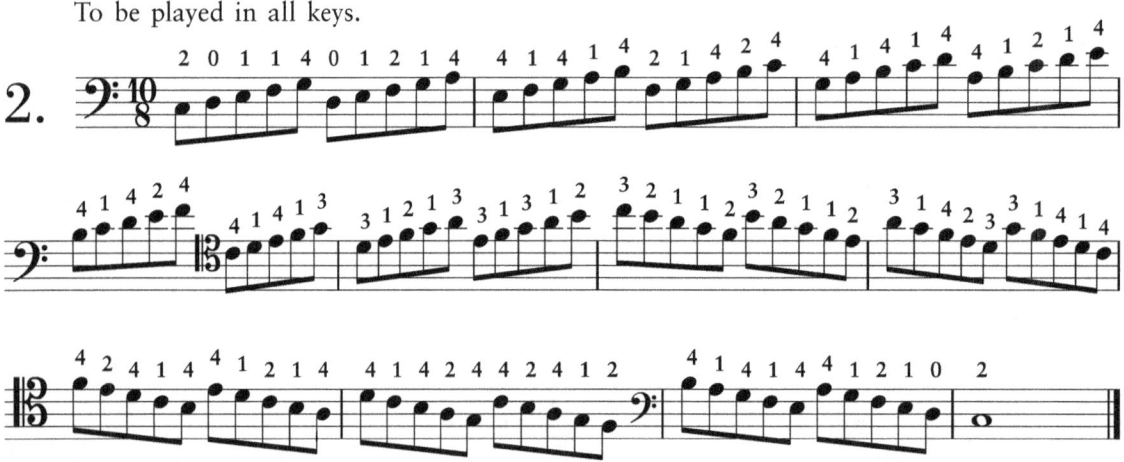

Perfecting Techniques through Employing Scales, Exercises, and Orchestral Excerpts

Related Orchestral Excerpts
(INCLUDING EXCERPTS REFERENCED IN BOWINGS SECTION)

> "ANCHOR" STROKES
> (V) Play note down-bow on string at frog
> (⊓) Play note up-bow on string at frog
> (×) Play note on string, lower half of bow

Beethoven I, 1st Movement

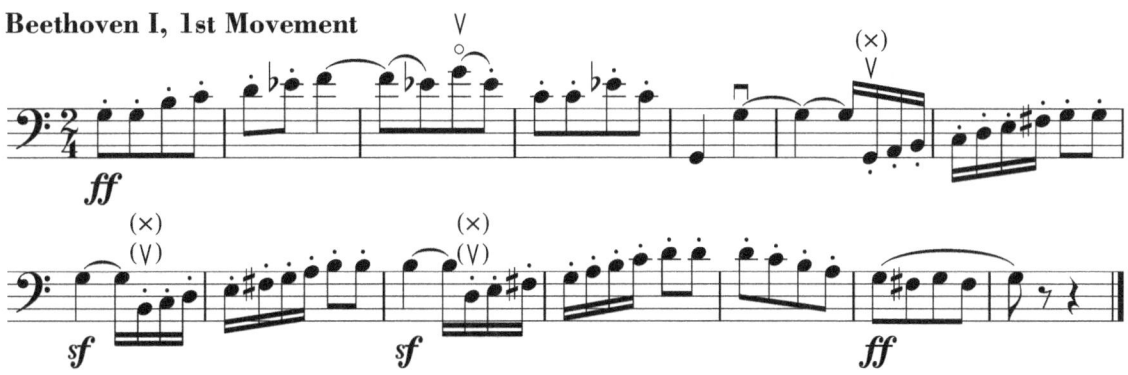

Beethoven III, 2nd Movement

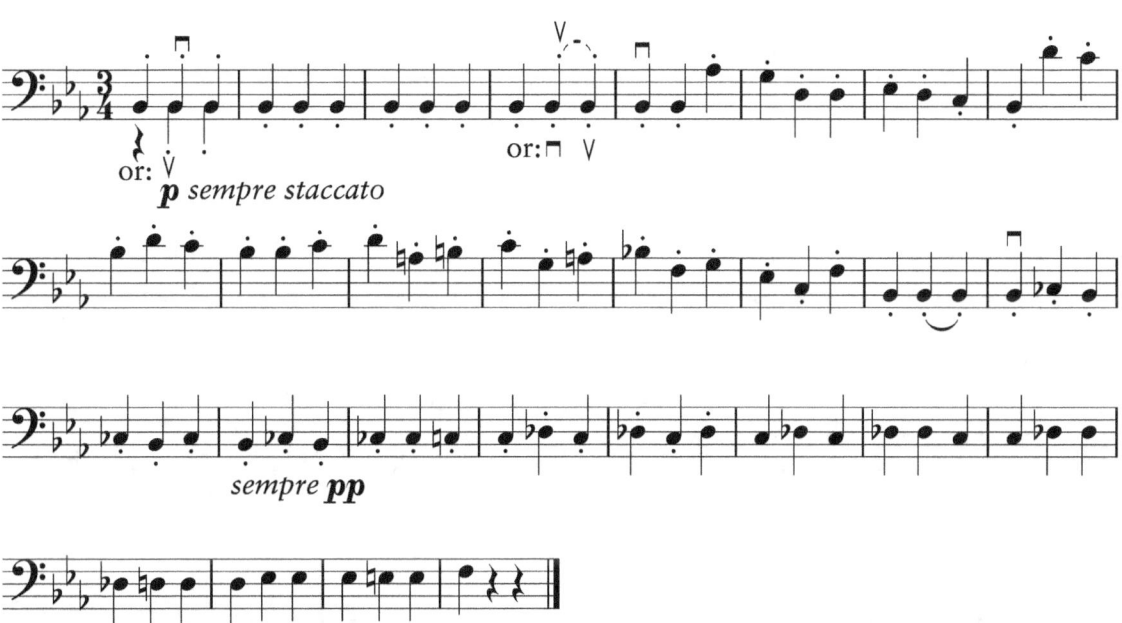

77

Perfecting Techniques through Employing Scales, Exercises, and Orchestral Excerpts

Beethoven V, 3rd Movement

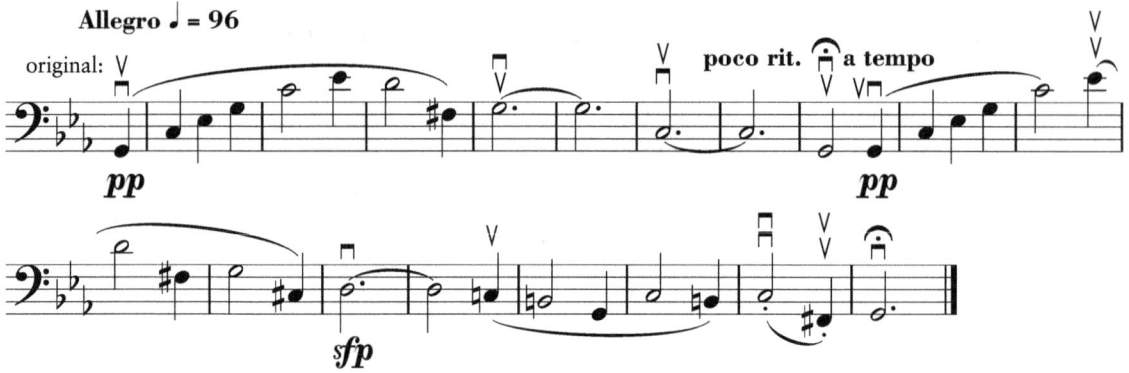

Beethoven V, 3rd Movement

Alternate bowing offered affords more natural rolling across strings (down-bow) than does the more common use of up-bow for the arpeggiated portion of this passage. It also eliminates the crescendo tendency" built into an up-bow stroke.

Beethoven V, 3rd Movement

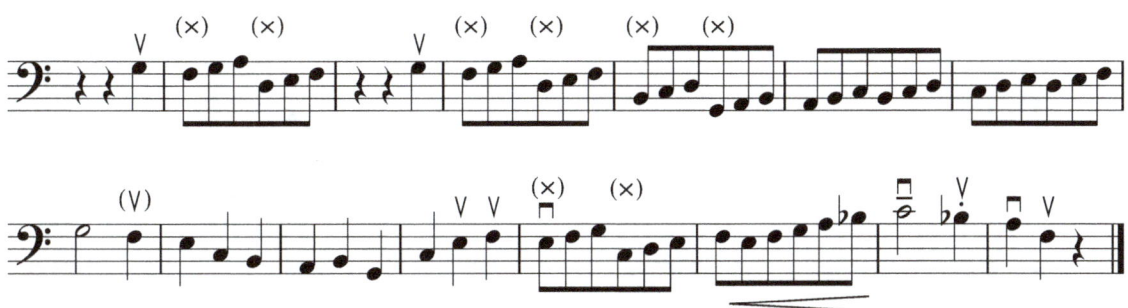

Although this passage is primarily played spiccato, there are symbols over certain notes that indicate a need for solid contact with the string, as there would be in playing that note "on the string." The result should be more bowing control and a clearer articulation of these notes (which often tend to lose their identity). This approach will also positively affect the clarity of notes immediately following notes in the passage.

Beethoven V, 4th Movement

In the second bar of above passage and in similar figures, the eighth notes should be played with a sharp staccato-like bite and slurs should also start with a bite. The sixth bar of this excerpt should start on string and continue with more of a staccato/spiccato-like effort than a pure spiccato. This is a good example of a passage that combines physical characteristics of both staccato and spiccato.

Beethoven VI, 4th Movement

The preceding Beethoven V example is really a reverse version of above bowing (except for rhythmic difference). All notes in this example are played with a moderate staccato.

Beethoven VII, 1st Movement

The main focus here should be bow recovery (back to frog area) before the down-bow sixteenths. This not only provides more articulation for these notes, but places the bow more meaningfully for the balance of following passage(s).

Beethoven VII, 3rd Movement

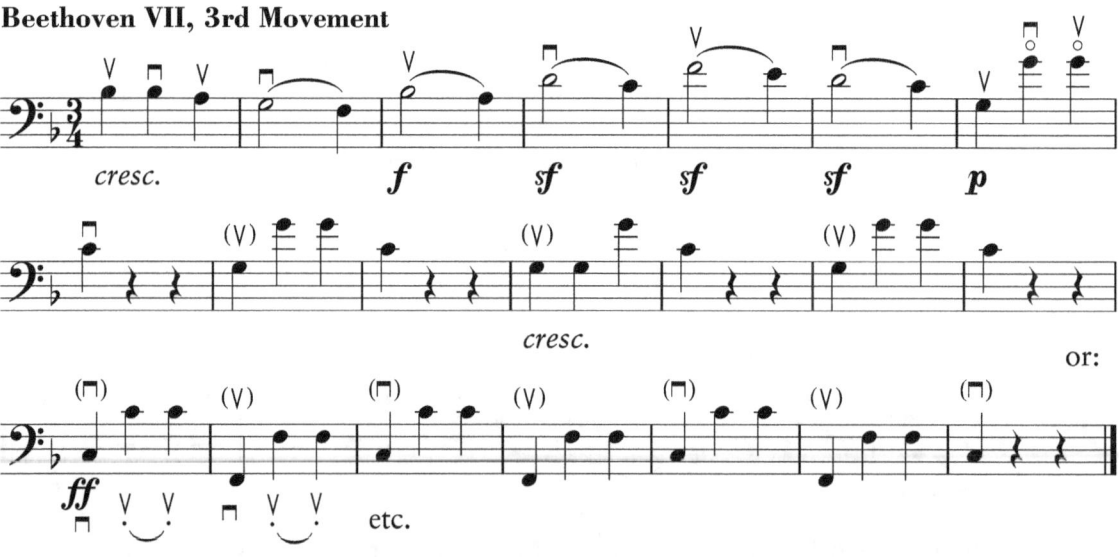

Although the resulting aural character should be that of a spiccato, octave skips should be started with bow on the string. This provides more bow control and clarity for octaves or other intervals when crossing two strings.

Perfecting Techniques through Employing Scales, Exercises, and Orchestral Excerpts

Beethoven VII, 4th Movement

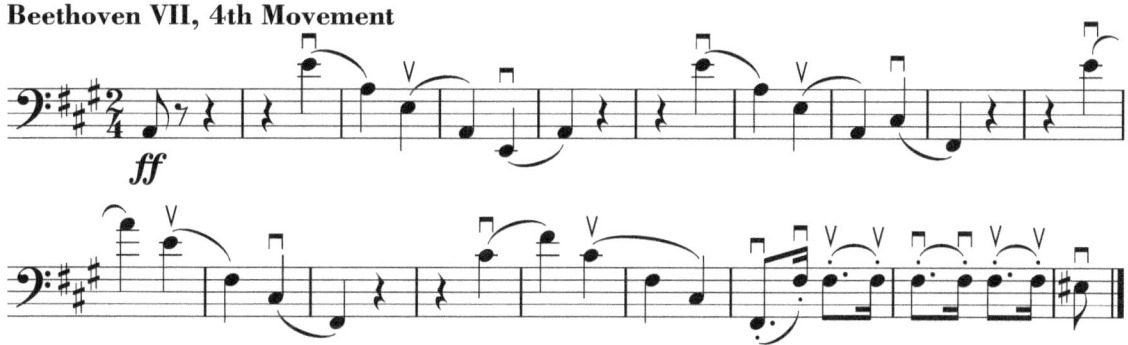

The bowing suggested (musically) relates to an articulated second beat. This emphasized phrasing is present throughout this movement. One need only to listen to the treatment of themes by upper strings, winds, and tympani to note the constant rhythmic and melodic presence of the articulated second beat.

There is no musical justification for the slurring of three or four notes in these figures. Slurring two notes rather than the three notes (seen in orchestra parts) also results in an increased sonority of the lowest notes.

Beethoven VIII, 1st Movement

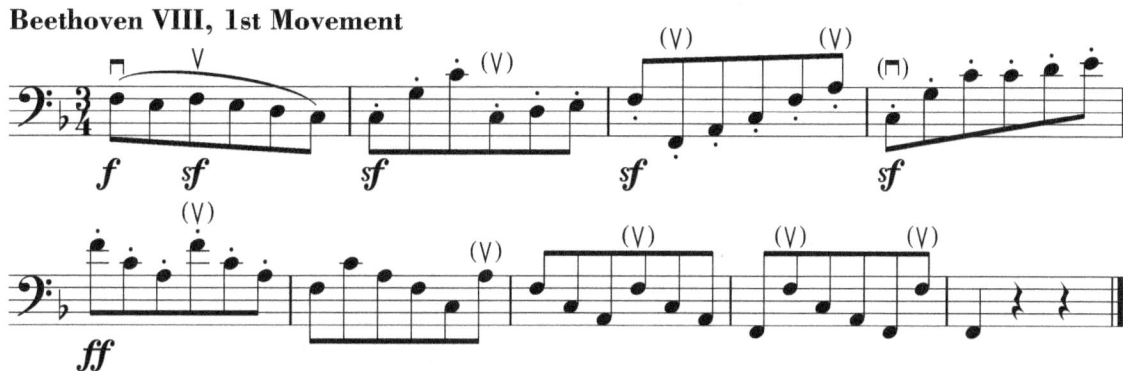

This passage is included to indicate "anchor" notes.

Perfecting Techniques through Employing Scales, Exercises, and Orchestral Excerpts

See text on following page for analysis of this recitative.

Beethoven IX, 4th Movement

Beethoven IX, 4th Movement, contd.

There is a great deal one can discuss about this recitative, but there are restrictions of how in depth a discussion can be when using only the printed page. The recitative has been subject to endless interpretations and, unfortunately, too many misinterpretations. Of course, one can respond "According to whom?" I will therefore try to do my best in providing logic for the observations I feel necessary to make.

Before the entrance of our (bass and cello) recitative, the full orchestra performs a very intense forte Presto introduction. Our entry needs to be a reply to the statement just made. The tempo marking has not changed. The nuance indicated is forte, and our only other indication is the marking "Recitativ." Is our reply one of apology to the challenging character of the orchestra statement or an intense rebuttal seemingly implied by the lack of any new tempo or nuance indication. Nothing printed implies anything other than the aggressive reply. This is another example of Beethoven's amazing ability to create dramatic energy.

This same general approach is in order until our entrance on the piano B-Flat after the two-bar rest in the andante cantabile. You will note the bowing indicated in the fifth-bar of our passage is a down-bow rather than the more usually employed up-bow. My reasoning is based on the intervals found in bar 7 (F# to C#) and bar 8 (A to B#), both reminiscent of the previous drama created by Beethoven's use of 4ths, 5ths, 6ths, and 7ths, always focal points at intense parts of a phrase. It seems that in keeping with the seemingly inferred importance of the phrasing of such intervals, employing the use of up-bow to a down-bow for these intervals of a 5th and 7th, encourages a lift or spacing in the sound that shadows the lift or space used for all of the preceding entries with similar intervals.

Following our three-bar rest in the allegro assai, we enter using the same interval as in our opening statement. Note that our tempo at this point is very close to that of the preceding Allegro Assai. This is another indication of the sense of motion (tempo) that Beethoven had in mind for all of our entrances in the recitative. Nothing notated in the recitative justifies some lugubrious renditions we have all heard from conductors great and small.

On the other hand, there is room for imagination and interpretation based on what seems clearly indicated by the tempos and nuances that do exist. There have been impressively imaginative and musical renditions of this wonderful moment for those of us in the bass clef.

Perfecting Techniques through Employing Scales, Exercises, and Orchestral Excerpts

Beethoven: *Leonore No. 3 Overture*

This excerpt is another example of Version B for bowings 16 and 17. It requires an articulated, measured slur and staccato-like eighth notes.

Berlioz: *Roman Carnival Overture*

Note bowing recommendation in second and third bar.

Berlioz: *Symphonie Fantastique*, 4th Movement

Perfecting Techniques through Employing Scales, Exercises, and Orchestral Excerpts

Be prepared to use either of the two bowings indicated. Bowing 1 of the above passage is being widely used by bass sections. It was originally all the other string sections that used this bowing, while the basses played the below hooked bowing.

Bowing 1 is played much more like two sixteenth notes, rather than a sixteenth to a (longer) dotted-eighth. This is a natural result of using the upper bowing. With tempo being very rapid, this result is acceptable. In essence, the bowing stroke sounds no different than playing the following figure:

Molto Allegro

Berlioz - *Symphonie Fantastique* "Witches Dance"

I believe the bowings recommended will provide more control, making it much easier to properly project passages in this section. It is essential that the bow be brought back to exact area of placement, indicated by anchor bowing markings.

85

Brahms I, 1st Movement

Practice the suggested bowings with the exact placement indicated and you will find it much easier to more clearly project and enunciate this passage and similar passages in this movement.

Brahms I, 4th Movement

Note the bowing used is to encourage aggressive articulation on notes they affect. I believe use of up-bow would not allow the strength of stroke required for these notes, provided by marked down-bows.

Note the anchor notes marked indicate replacing stroke at frog before continuing. This provides uniformity of length and character of stroke.

Brahms II, 1st Movement

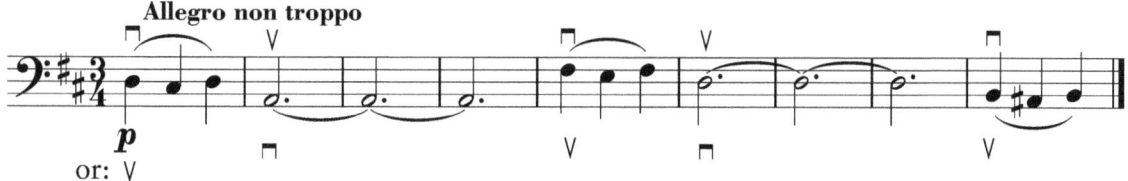

The bowing one chooses depends on the phrasing implied by a conductor (for the first two measures).

To help you determine your own preference of phrasing, listen to the section later in the movement, where the woodwinds lead in development of this theme. You will find they use the three-quarter notes as a lead-in to the dotted half note. I believe this is indeed the route to follow for the whole movement. Note: the conductors have never criticized this woodwind interpretation, yet generally make no effort to maintain or request the same phrasing for the opening bars or other like musical statements in the movement.

Brahms II, 4th Movement

The bowing suggested in the pp section is not the same as printed version. I would, however, suggest playing it through several times until you are comfortably familiar with this different bowing approach. I think you will find it flows more easily for technical execution. There are numerous times printed bowings have been altered in orchestral violin parts by concertmasters and others. It needs to be realized how multi-detailed it is to create an orchestral work and score that dots all the i's and crosses all the t's. One could wonder if composers' indications are really beyond

Perfecting Techniques through Employing Scales, Exercises, and Orchestral Excerpts

critical examination. If the composer was primarily a pianist, would his judgment be infallible for marking string parts? Was an alternate bowing ever proposed to the composer? There is no question that some passages would be and have been open to discussion by string section leaders and soloists. I have been present during the preparation of a new orchestral works with composers present, when conductors pose questions about markings in the score. Composers often reply, "Feel free to change it if it works better." Of course, this is not a license for a free-for-all, but it does indicate that there can be room for negotiation, and not everything on paper is written in stone, nor necessarily the only version acceptable to the composer. I honestly believe that if Brahms could hear the suggested alternative, it might please him. In any case, one must of course practice and be prepared to play the printed version, as this is a very commonly used audition passage.

Mozart #35, 1st Movement

The above excerpt is included to indicate a suggested bowing. In addition, it is advisable to play a measured trill (in length) in order to allow comfortable rhythmic execution of the two sixteenth notes that follow.

The next excerpt from this movement is again an example of a sharply articulated and measured slur, allowing for clarity of execution of notes and rhythms.

Mozart #35, 1st Movement

Perfecting Techniques through Employing Scales, Exercises, and Orchestral Excerpts

Mozart #35, 4th Movement

Mozart #35, 4th Movement

Rarely has the fp starting in the fifth measure of this excerpt been successfully played by a string section. It may never be played successfully; however, I have stumbled on a thought process that can hopefully bring more success for some of us. I therefore suggest that you first play the passage in tempo, as softly and clearly as possible without any fp or accent. Now repeat this at least 5–10 times. Then totally erase from the mind the thought of fp and play the passage in tempo, as pp as possible. Then think only of an accent on the first of every four notes. Make a very short accent on first of every four notes, and not a fp, maintaining the pp for the other portions of the passage. If successful, you will have achieved or come closer to the audible result of an fp. I don't know why the mind responds this way, but in working with students, the mental gymnastic has usually improved the results.

Perfecting Techniques through Employing Scales, Exercises, and Orchestral Excerpts

Mozart #39, 1st Movement

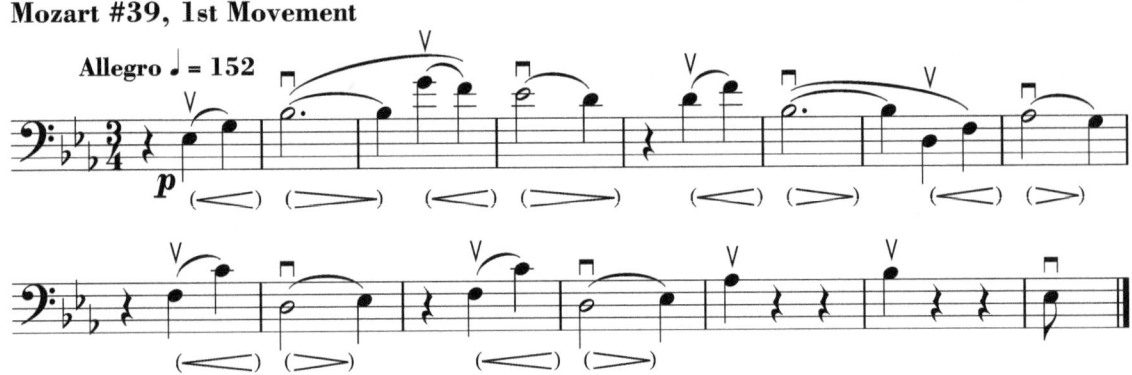

Mozart #39, 1st Movement

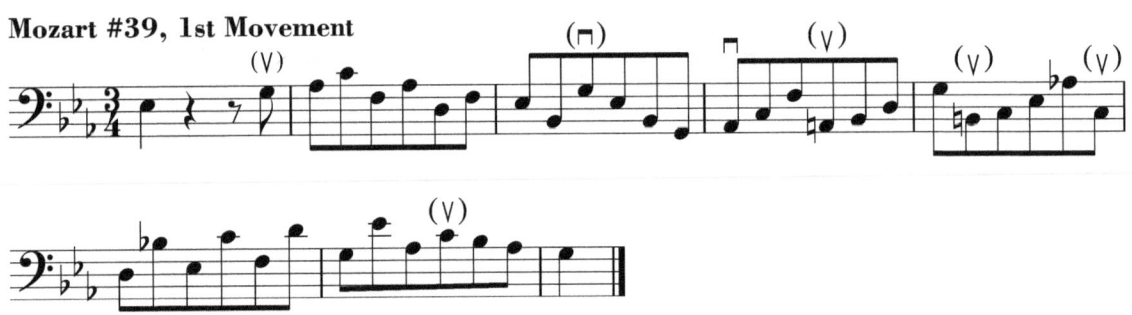

The whole string section repeats this phrase a number of times. The constant flaw of the surging up-bow reaching a louder peak than the coming down-bow resolution on the downbeat of every even-numbered bar is unfortunately universal. Marked in parenthesis, you will find phrasing indications. I believe most will agree with this conclusion, but in performance, the surging up-bow actually violates desirable phrasing.

It needs to be stated here that the surging up-bow is a constant violation of phrasing by string instrumentalists. It is usually a result of the note value of an up-bow being shorter than preceding stroke. For example:

In both examples, the down-bow is longer in metric duration than the up-bow. The tendency is to rush the up-bow preparing for the next down-bow and, in the process, not only speed up the up-bow but also increase the volume. In order to avoid this when speeding up the bow, decrease the pressure and limit speed, so that an unwanted surge does not occur. The habit of surging is universal and takes place not only in student orchestras but also in our nation's top orchestras. The surprising part is that almost all conductors accept this practice, allowing improper phrasing to go unnoticed.

In the second excerpt from this movement, you will note my anchor symbol for reasserting firm contact with the string. I describe these specially marked pitches as "anchor" notes; a place where one resecures the bow stroke in a part of a passage that requires additional bowing security for articulation. These are points in the passage that when played purely as a high bouncing spiccato will cause discomfort in crossing strings. This results in less clearly executed neighboring notes.

As in many allegro movements using this bowing (two slurred notes and two separate strokes or the reverse of this pattern), it is important to realize that the slur is articulated with the same emphasis as the separate strokes. It is important that the slur be measured and not elongated, allowing time and space to articulate the next stroke.

The slur mark is not definitive in and of itself. It is interpreted in length and articulation by the character of the music and the figures surrounding it. A slur does not mean anything except to bind notes together. It does not necessarily mean a legato articulation. That is determined by the character of the phrase.

Mozart #40, 1st Movement

In this excerpt, too often, we again experience the surging up-bow. It is musically more appropriate for the quarter note on the downbeat to be the focal note, without surging or overshadowing being caused by the up-bow.

You will note here again the special marking of anchor strokes that secure controlled articulation (after string changes).

Mozart #40, 4th Movement

This famous audition passage has been partially discussed in the written section of this book. Be very diligent about making the bowing in the third and fifth bars being very articulated (including slurs). Following that you will again see markings for anchor notes, which help control a clear articulation.

Perfecting Techniques through Employing Scales, Exercises, and Orchestral Excerpts

Mozart #41, 1st Movement

As in many passages similar to the first and fifth bars, some pitches tend to get aurally lost. There are technical efforts we can make to achieve more projection of clarity. The problem often stems from note(s) that get neglected because of their position in the passage or a change of strings that doesn't clearly articulate. In the first bar, the problem is the string change on an open string. We usually fail to focus on making the A string sound and simply rush past it. If we analyze the passage, we realize that the G will sound, as it is our opening articulation. The B has an advantage as it is a fingered note being more likely to respond than the open A. The C will definitely sound, being the last note in the figure. Our focus then is to make sure the open A sounds. Use some restriction on the bow speed on the open A and feel firm contact with the string as you play it. Sit on the A and don't rush by it.

In the fifth bar, it is the E that will likely not clearly articulate. Even though it is fingered, we rush by it in anxious anticipation of making the shift to the F#. Focus on the E as a pressure point and avoid just sliding by it.

Why make the effort to discuss these universally "sloughed" figures? There are many such figures, which we can execute more clearly with a little analysis. It doesn't require as much practice as does being consciously analytical. In this way you can find solutions to many passages, for which we previously accepted compromise.

Mozart #41, 1st Movement

For this excerpt, again note the anchor strokes.

Perfecting Techniques through Employing Scales, Exercises, and Orchestral Excerpts

Mozart #41, 4th Movement

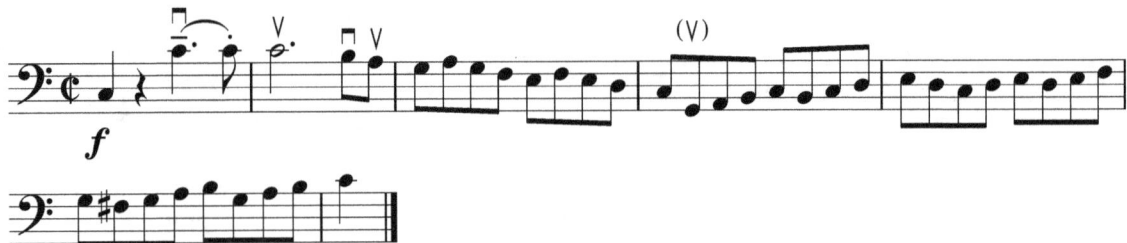

The eighths in the second bar are marked as they appear in the score and are most often played without a slur. The printed bowing is the most used and desirable.

Mozart #41, 4th Movement

The trills in this excerpt often create discomfort and sound disorganized. Perform them at the fastest speed you are capable of and for a specifically measured time value. This will allow you to finish (stop) trill in time to make the shift and clearly articulate the following eighth note. Reiterating, the trill must be measured both in speed and length to allow for clarity of rhythm on the eighth note leading to half-note.

Mozart #41, 4th Movement

Again heed the significance of anchor notes for the above excerpt.

Mozart #41, 4th Movement

In this excerpt, we again have rapidly moving pick-up notes to a resolution note on the downbeat. I have discussed an approach for more clarity in these types of pick-up notes. There is an additional challenge here in the form of the irregular rhythms of the pick-up notes. There are triplets and quadruplets. Reduced, they are either equal to an

Perfecting Techniques through Employing Scales, Exercises, and Orchestral Excerpts

eighth note or a quarter note in value. Note that there are two-bar rhythmic sequences of each rhythmic figure, except for first and last figures (which are both equal to an eighth-note value). First practice the rhythmic aspect by playing the full value of the figure as either an eighth note or a quarter note. After you become comfortable with the rhythmic pattern of the rests and value of the figures, practice the passage with all pitches and figures as written.

Schubert IX, 1st Movement

Schubert IX, 4th Movement

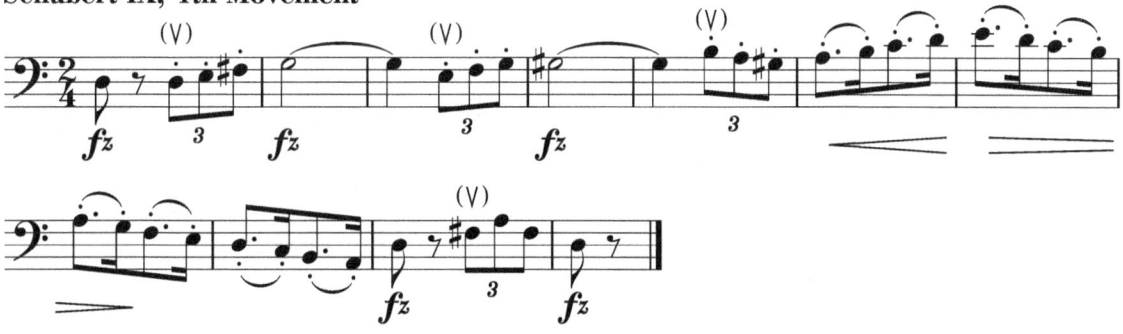

Schubert IX, 4th Movement

Both excerpts of the fourth movement of the Schubert IX are based on examples 20–23 in the section "Essential Bowings to Use Scales." See the instructions on p. 36 for suggestions on the articulation of bowing involved.

Perfecting Techniques through Employing Scales, Exercises, and Orchestral Excerpts

Smetana: *The Bartered Bride Overture*

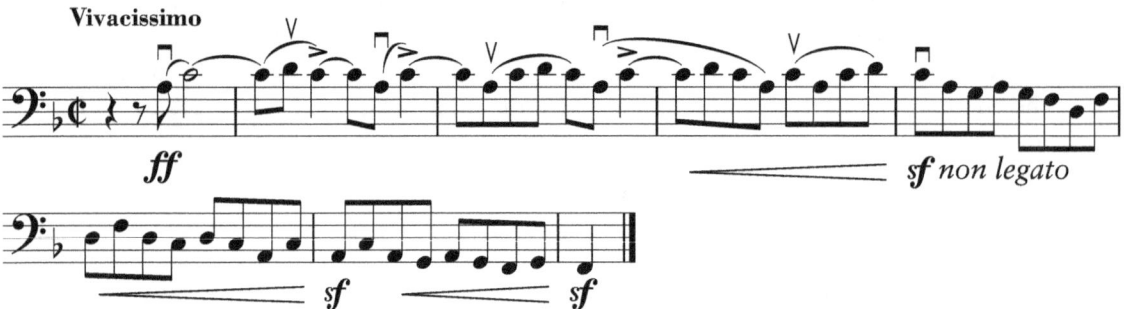

A very challenging passage with an awkward bowing. A somewhat altered bowing is suggested, which may help, but doesn't eliminate the fact that the passage remains awkward for bowing.

Strauss: *Also Sprach Zarathustra*

Strauss: *Also Sprach Zarathustra*

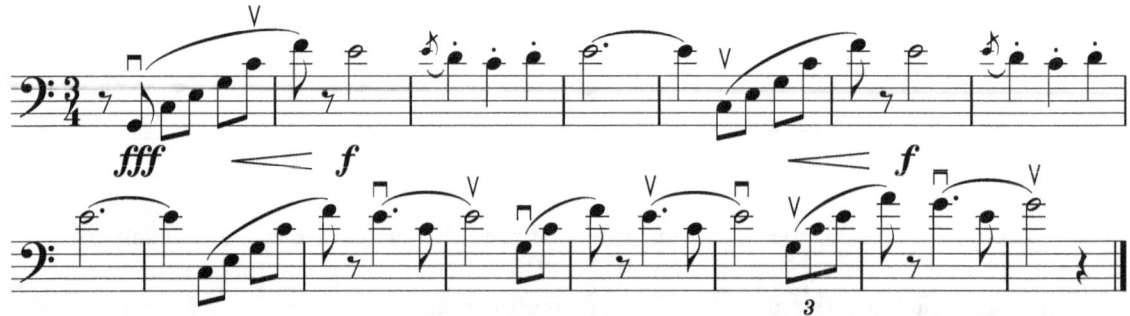

A suggestion for bowing is the prime reason for inclusion of both of these excerpts.

Perfecting Techniques through Employing Scales, Exercises, and Orchestral Excerpts

Strauss: *Don Juan*

Although this passage is generally played with a spiccato stroke very close to the string, note the indicated anchor notes. This anchor placement will provide needed control and bowing articulation.

Strauss: *Ein Heldenleben*

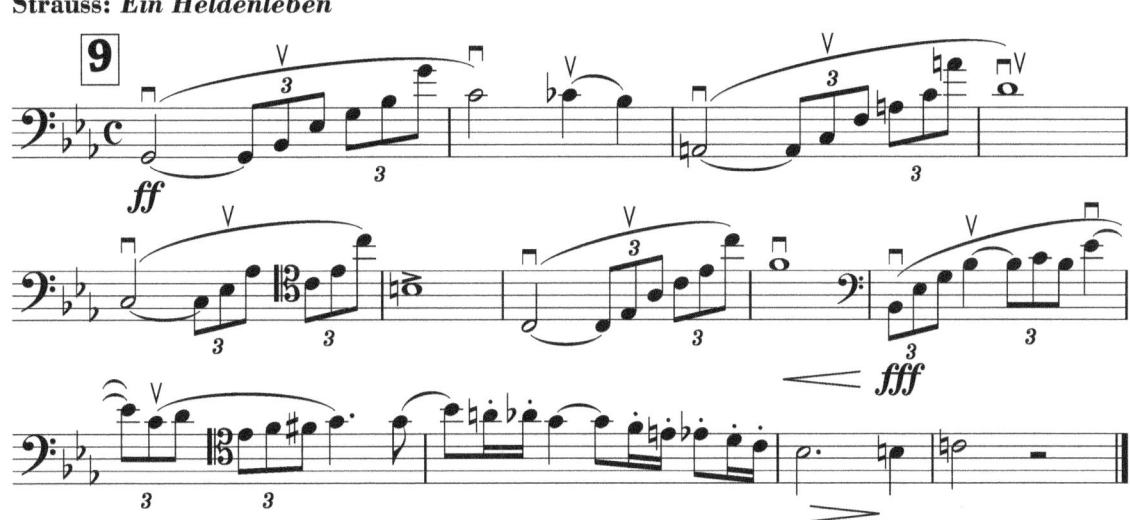

Rarely are the triplets clearly enunciated in this excerpt. This is more often due to mistreatment of the passage rather than the available technical ability to create clarity.

The first triplet is usually rushed and thus not clearly enunciated. To improve the result, practice only playing the following, until the triplet is clearly audible and a feeling of solid, deliberate rhythm is established.

When the first part of the passage is comfortable, practice the following second part:

After each part of the passage has become comfortable, play the complete passage:

(continued on next page)

Perfecting Techniques through Employing Scales, Exercises, and Orchestral Excerpts

(continued from previous page)

Use the same approach for practicing the five arpeggios that are in this excerpt. You may find that using the suggested process may be necessary for more than one practice session on this excerpt. Keep in mind that it is rarely the second part of the arpeggio that is unclear, as rushing usually takes place on the first arpeggio triplet. (Use a metronome, clicking quarter beats and focus on arriving perfectly on the third beat before completing the whole passage.)

Strauss: *Ein Heldenleben*

This excerpt is included to offer a bowing that should provide more control of tone and dynamics.

Strauss: *Ein Heldenleben*

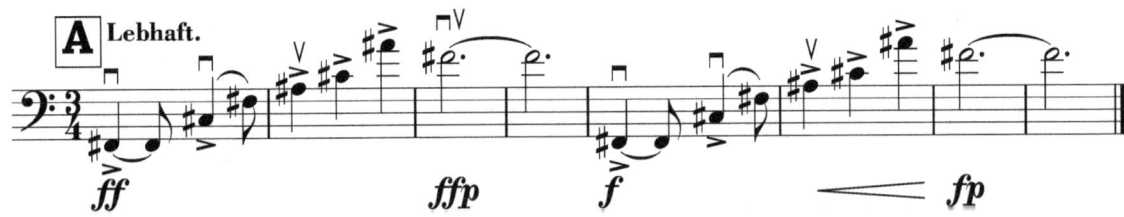

This "Lebhaft" section contains a bowing suggestion that should provide more control of bowing articulation and tonal qualities.

Tchaikovsky: "Trepak" from *The Nutcracker Suite*)

This excerpt illustrates Bowings 13–17 on p. 33–35. In bars 5, 6, and 13–16, again keep the eighth-note length restricted in order to allow comfortable articulation of sixteenth notes.

Tchaikovsky: *Romeo and Juliet*

Tchaikovsky: *Romeo and Juliet*

This excerpt is an example of bowings 13–17 on p. 33–35.

Tchaikovsky IV, 1st Movement

The predominant bowing in this excerpt is similar to that given in Beethoven's Symphony no. 7. Although the rhythmic placement within the beat is different, the actual bowing is based on the sixteenth hooked to the eighth, as it is in Beethoven's VII, first movement.

Weber: Euryanthe Overture

Assai moderato

The problem in this passage is primarily bowing a complex combination of string crossings. Again, we can employ some mental/physical gymnastics to cure this, using the following approach to practicing this passage.

Break up the triplet eighth-notes into two groups and practice them in the following manner:

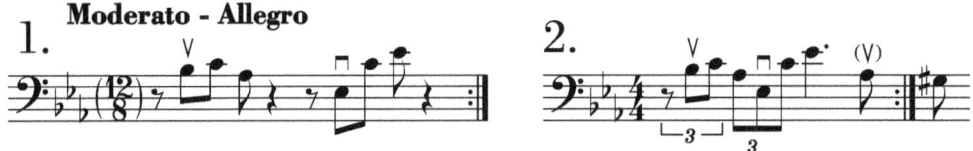

Play firmly on the string, with deliberate articulations, and for now without using any bounce of the bow. The inserted rest is where the awkward crossing would take place, but we are eliminating that mentally for the moment. Play this pattern at first slowly, repeating it as indicated, and then gradually increase tempo as you get comfortable with the bowing indicated. Make sure that the first eighth-note B and the eighth-note (lower) E are played firmly on the string.

Now, think of the bowing as two separate efforts, and play the original printed passage plus the first note of the following bar. Play in a moderate tempo, still retaining the bowing division in your mind, as shown in the practice pattern. Gradually increase tempo, but keep focusing on the passage as being two separate efforts (patterns of motion).

If you have succeeded in the mental division of the passage as suggested, the bowing obstacle to playing the passage should be resolved, since we have eliminated the awkward string-crossing maneuver.

PART 3

Informative Essays for Double Bassists

"Basses, You Are Late."

Are the Conductors possibly right? Do basses really sound late in orchestral playing?

Through constant and careful listening to live and recorded performances, I must admit there are times when the double basses do sound late.

At times it is possibly an illusion caused by the fact that our instruments resonate longer than other string instruments, causing us to be heard a bit longer than the other string instruments. This also could create the impression that we are playing behind the others.

At other times, however, our instruments do sound later or behind. Listen carefully to attacks, spiccato, short chords in orchestral fortes, etc. I am now convinced that since we have much thicker and longer strings, plus bows that are relatively light, our strings can physically respond a fraction of a second later, causing us to sound late. It is not that we play later than anyone else, but our instrument (at times) may respond slower. Is there a cure? Think of the tubist, contrabassoonist, French hornist, and all of the instruments where there is delay in sound between the player's initial effort and the instrument's actual sound response, and you have a clue to our solution. They don't consciously come in early to create the sound on time, but over years of playing they have instinctively learned to make their physical effort so that the sound is produced to coincide with other orchestral sections.

As bassists we need to develop the same instinct. We must learn to make our physical effort so that the string speaks exactly when necessary. In order to coincide with the pulse, this has to become an instinct and not a practice of anticipation. We are actually doing this when we play pizzicato. We don't release the string until the right moment to blend with the other instruments. We need to do the same with bowing. I believe mere awareness of when you are producing the sound can over time cause one to instinctively adjust to producing sound, which will coincide with the sound production of the rest of the ensemble.

Chamber Music

**AN EXCELLENT VEHICLE FOR MUSICAL
AND TECHNICAL EVALUATION AND GROWTH**

Unfortunately, as bassists, our opportunities to play chamber music are very limited. This genre provides a rare experience of being the only bassist, allowing us to critically hear every note and stroke we play. We will be paired with the other string instruments in a setting where we must learn to blend the sound of the bass with the other strings. Everything one plays in this setting is exposed and requires more attention and perfection. Intonation has to be precise and, most important, all phrases and accompaniment must be shaped to blend with the musical expressiveness of the group.

There is a sensitivity one can develop in performing chamber music that is not duplicated in any other setting. The sound with which we play may have to be altered from other forms of music making in order to achieve the quality of sound that blends in a chamber-music setting.

Take and make every opportunity you can to play chamber music. I was privileged early in my career to be able to play classical string trios and quartets with very fine violinists and violists by taking the place of a cellist. If you can find musical friends who will put up with you playing the cello parts on the double bass, it can be a great experience. Whenever realistic, play the cello part an octave higher than written; allowing us to play (in this kind of setting) in the octave in which the cellist would sound when reading the same music.

Aside from the learning that can take place through playing chamber music, there is a musical satisfaction to be experienced that is quite unique. This is also a rare opportunity to play some of the greatest works of the Classical period.

French Bow vs. German Bow

Time and discussion eventually bares all the attitudes and ignorance present on this probably unnecessary subject.

I have taught both French and German bow. I spent a short period in my earliest studies playing French bow and afterward played the German bow. Why? Because I had to change teachers, and my first teacher taught French bow and my second teacher taught only the German bow. Therefore, I studied German bow much longer, resulting in my primarily playing with the German bow. At that point, I had no experience that caused me to have any preference for either school of bowing, as I was still a musical infant. Now that I have years of experience in both teaching and performing, I still have no preference.

In the third year of my students' undergraduate study (while I was teaching at Indiana University), they would spend a whole semester studying the "other" school of bowing. German bow students would study French bow and vice versa. Since the similarities between the bows are really greater than the differences, students adapted to the "new bow" experience quickly. They learned all the basic bowing strokes, good sound production, and all essential elements necessary to actually perform with the new bow.

Students started out by only practicing scales and bowings with the new bow, playing everything else with their native bow. By the end of the semester, they would study exercises and more with the new bow. Some were so taken with the experience that they desired to become equally proficient with both bows. A fine young bassist with excellent playing skills using his original school of bowing totally switched to the new bow because he believed he was more comfortable playing with it. I felt this was quite unnecessary, since he was so proficient with his original type of bow. He actually became principal bass in one of our country's fine orchestras, using the bow to which he converted.

I find no real difference in a student's basic results with one bow over the other. In fact, studying the new bow requires going through the learning process for bowing all over again. This brings a renewed consciousness of bowing techniques, which students instinctively transfer to their native school of bowing. There is a new clarity about their process of bowing that results from this conscious reevaluation of the techniques of bowing. This experience should also make them better teachers.

Are there differences between French and German schools of bowing? Yes, there are. Slurring across two strings (or string crossing) is easier with the French bow, which allows the horizontal use of the wrist to help this maneuver. There may be an advantage in initially producing a fuller sound with the German bow, which in the beginning allows attaining leverage more easily. In the end, however, examples of the finest double bass playing include both French and German bow players. Currently, there are more French bow players than German, and so statistically, there are probably more fine players around who play French bow. There were times in the past where the situation was reversed or close to even. At certain points in history, you would find Germany, Austria, some Slavic countries, Hungary, etc. contained mostly German bow bassists. On the other hand, France, Italy, England, Belgium, etc. had mostly had French bow bassists. After World War II, the German bow began to lose favor in Europe as a probable result of political and ideologic attitudes. I spent six months in Denmark (1963–64), which had been occupied by Germany in World War II. As I remember, the members of the Danish National Radio Orchestra were all French bow players. Many had studied in France. No one had studied in Germany, which was just across their southern border. The resentment of the German occupation during World War II left formerly occupied nations in Western Europe with populations that largely avoided personal contact with the Germanic nations. This left countries where the French school was the primary one being taught or played. The result was and is a predominance of players using French bow today in Europe and North America.

This did not happen in the former Soviet Union, which had limited contact with Western Europe, resulting in a predominance of Soviet bassists using the German bow. This is also true of Slavic nations, which were dominated by the Soviet Union.

I was once in conversation with one of the most respected conductors of the twentieth century (under whom I previously had the privilege of playing), who was offering me a position in his current orchestra. He asked, "By the way, I don't remember, do you play French or German bow?" When I replied "German," he expressed a hearty, "Good! Now we will have four French bow players and four German bow players in the section." How much more of a perfect reply could there be to the nonsensical question of the superiority of either school of bowing, than realizing that equal representation provides a desirable balance..

Auditions and Recitals

AUDITION MATERIALS, ATTITUDE (NERVES), PREPARATION, "AUDITIONING FOR EXPERIENCE"

Personal make-up relative to public solo performance, be it recitals, auditions, etc., creates a different spectrum of innate behavior for those who thrive on performing than others who shudder at the thought of performing solo in public.

Those who thrive playing in front of others need not read further. They have no concern other than having to be properly prepared musically and technically. For the rest of us, first we must be extremely well prepared, so that if we play less than our best, it will still be musically and technically positive. How do we achieve this? There are no guarantees that I am aware of, but I do know that failing to do well in public performance, when well prepared, is largely due to having our concentration and awareness being overly focused on nervousness.

Although we need to acknowledge that nerves may play a part in our public performance, we must not consciously dwell on whether or not we are nervous. We must accept and allow that to unfold as it will, as we have other things to which we must give our attention. Do your best to focus on performing as well as you can by trying to put into play all the learning you have achieved with the solo or orchestral excerpt.

Concentrate on mentally visualizing what you have learned that is required technically and musically in order to play the music in front of you. Have your inner ear imagining the passage exactly as you would like to perform it.

If you are playing an audition and have prepared as intelligently as you can, there is nothing more you can do at that point. Being worried or nervous will make nothing better. You are playing in front of other humans who understand nervousness and are hoping to find a competent player to join their orchestra. It is not to their advantage to scare everyone into playing poorly or becoming nervous. All one can do is try to do one's best. Thinking about being nervous means you are not really thinking or focusing as much as you can on playing. Concentrating on one's nervousness deflects one's concentration from one's true goal. This is not only an affliction musicians suffer, but is quite universal for most professions where some sort of solo public performing is required. (Let's hope it is not true for surgeons.)

Relative to all this, there is an incident I experienced that is a perfect example of how faulty concentration can create failure. I was in the final round of an important orchestral audition. For the first round, I was normally nervous but remained focused. In the final round everything was going fine until I realized that I wasn't at all nervous. My focus immediately became centered on why or how strange it was that I wasn't nervous. Didn't I always get nervous? My focus on playing vanished. Of course, nerves then took over, as that was where I was focused. Of course my resulting performance made much less of an impression than of what I was capable.

This experience did not cure me of nervousness, but it was the beginning of the realization that being nervous was not my goal in performing and that one needs to have one's mind properly focused on one's playing. Nerves will take care of themselves. They don't need our conscious attention. These realizations worked for me. I taught myself to accept whatever my nerves were up to and managed to keep my focus on the challenge of playing, most often with satisfying results.

Thoughts Concerning Teaching

Teachers must be able to communicate ideas, instill confidence, inspire achievement, and provide reasoning for advising the use of performance practices we propose or insist upon.

No two people or students are alike. Teachers have to develop a various ways to express or explain the same thought or idea. Communication with those seeking to learn means expressing thoughts that can translate so that each student can comprehend. A single approach used to express an idea may not be totally comprehendible to all students. It is possible that a student may not have the capacity to absorb an idea, but it is more often the instructor's failure to intellectually connect with that student. I am sure we have all had occasions when, hearing someone explain something to us, we ponder, "What did he mean?" That implies that the words or approach used for communication didn't make the thought clear enough for some of us to understand. Yet others hearing the same expression of the thought understood what it was all about. Although we might feel somewhat inadequate when we don't understand a teacher, it is probably something in one's background that is different in some way than others hearing the same thought. This difference of perception, or personal evolution of forms of comprehension, could short-circuit the message for some of us, but not others. It can take different cues for different individuals to understand the same message.

In teaching the double bass, I have had students open a door, use the bow on strings pretending they were sawing wood, practice the act of sitting down or standing up from a chair, relate to the stances of boxers, leaning and pressing hands against a wall, and use many other ideas or props which involved experienced behaviors that could be related to some aspect of playing the bass. Proper teaching involves including known behavior and its relationship to the "new" behavior being proposed. Why are large lecture-type classes so often difficult to grasp completely? They are tailored to express ideas, without complete concern about all of the audience's ability for comprehension of the form in which the thoughts are presented. There is often no opportunity for detailed questioning, even though not everyone in that audience has the background that allows total comprehension.

Private studio instruction must not allow a student to misunderstand or not comprehend the instruction given. The teacher must find varied means of transmitting knowledge or ideas so that every student can understand the instruction being given. It may take specific tailoring instruction for the student who needs ideas expressed in his or her vernacular. Each person's background and ability to conceive ideas is unique.

In the public schools some teachers rely on a teaching plan for each day of instruction. As music teachers providing individual instruction, we must have an intellectual plan for each student that will best educate him or her. One approach does not fit all. Each of us has a general overall method of teaching applied music, but within that teaching pattern must be flexibility that allows our instructions to successfully reach each student.

Thoughts Concerning Directions for a Professional Career

PLAYING IN A SYMPHONY VS. POPULAR MUSIC GROUPS

When one has the ability to succeed in either pop or classical field of performance, one is usually mostly influenced by the form of music that seems more interesting, challenging, or musically energizing. Few think of the path of life each may provide.

Many years ago, I had the choice to join a big name band or remaining in the symphonic field. It struck me that most of my friends who took the direction of popular music were traveling much of the time and not around their families as often as those in symphony orchestras. Having experienced life with bands, I found I did not enjoy a life where you end up in town after town (interesting or not), living in a hotel with little opportunity for being productive during the daylight hours and playing the same tunes every night.

There was no question that I wanted a home and loved travel, but travel on my own terms and to areas that were of interest to me. I enjoy the preparation of at least one new program weekly with the musical and technical challenges, which is the life of a symphony musician. I still love the big bands of the '40s, '50s, and '60s. I have recordings of Kenton, Ellington, Basie, and Finnegan that I thoroughly enjoy. However, I am pleased that I chose the symphony orchestra as my means of making music, allowing a lifestyle that made possible more normal family involvement and the musical challenges of the symphonic literature.

I am certainly not advocating this choice for all musical performers. I use myself as an example and indicate why I made my choice. Each musician has his or her own reasoning for the life he or she will choose to follow as well and the musical organization that will be most rewarding. I have many friends and former students who are happy successful bassists in bands and jazz groups around the country. They enjoy what they are doing as much I enjoyed my paths in music. I only suggest that one should consider the totality of life experience when choosing the path in music one wishes to follow. The choice of a musical path provides not only a direction for making music but also a way of life that goes with that musical experience.

Music Education for Public School Music Teaching

Prepare yourself to accept the probability that a formal degree in music education can be sadly lacking in equipping you properly for the teaching of strings. Public school music teachers should be well-trained, competent musicians and must not be subject to only a second-class musical education. Unfortunately, higher education often provides this second-class musical education for many choosing the bachelor's of music education degree.

The degree requirements for music education majors are heavily laden with how-to and theoretical courses requiring many credit hours, leaving too few for an adequate education in applied music areas. Why should a music-ed student need less applied instruction than an instrumental music major? There is so much less instrumental instruction, in fact, that they get about one-third the credit hours in applied music as an instrumental music major. This often results in officially assigning one-third of the practice time assigned to instrumental majors. The outcome frequently results in music education majors studying with a graduate assistant since major faculty shy away from students with very limited practice time. Limited practice time and limited instruction produces many music-ed students who become modest achievers in their major applied area and often lack the musical growth that their profession requires.

This result comes from the flawed conclusion of some faculties that a student pursuing a degree in music education does not need as much competency in their major applied area as instrumental majors. Often this means less comprehension in performance and acquired knowledge for the teaching of strings.

Even though these students may not have to achieve the upper levels of accomplished performance required of the instrumental major in order to acquire the teaching knowledge they need, current requirements are far too modest to provide for the musical needs of music-ed students. If we are going to have properly qualified string teachers for public school music teaching, they must be sufficiently competent on their concentration instrument. This requires more practice time and instruction from faculty rather than teaching assistants. The more one studies and performs, the more advanced techniques become and with that, hopefully more in-depth learning. An hour a day of practice five days a week and instruction from less than the most experienced faculty available does not provide the musical background to produce properly trained instrumental teachers.

Not only is the educational balance for the music education student out of kilter, but their credit hours required for graduation are often significantly higher than those required by other music degrees. This again legislates against this group of students having enough hours in the day to learn enough in their most critical areas of study. Being unnecessarily overburdened by course work defeats the learning process. We all have a limit to the amount of learning that can be achieved in a given period. Going beyond that limit creates a waste of time and effort.

Another element of educating these students is the study of secondary instruments, usually called String Techniques. The notion that one who is to be teacher can learn enough about the other members of the string family, through a heterogeneous grouping is nonsense. The majority of physically inept high-school bass students I have seen during my visits to public schools attest to the limited knowledge the string instrument teachers have attained about teaching or playing the double bass. This is one result of inadequate instruction in secondary instruments provided by the 'traditional' String Techniques class.

Am I advocating homogeneous classes? No! I simply reiterate that you can't pass on enough information to a class of 6–12 students in one or two class lessons a week to prepare qualified music teachers to for all stringed instruments. An argument I was given against individual instruction was that Music Education students must learn how to teach in a heterogeneous class situation and that the class method at the college level should fulfill that need. This is not very valid if the results are future teachers who don't know enough about their primary subject areas to competently instruct.

Having the opportunity to take over a String Techniques program for two years, I instituted a regimen whereby violin and viola string concentrations would be required to take one semester each of private cello and double bass. Cellists would similarly study double bass and violin. Double bassists would study violin and cello. All instruction consisted of weekly, one- hour private lessons. The results were beyond what was envisioned. Before the end of the semester, cellists and violinists (violists) alike developed really good bow arms and were playing competently into thumb position on the double bass. Similarly, double bassists achieved competency on cello and violin. The third semester of String Techniques was used for surveying methods, playing through Music Education materials for class string ensembles, and pedagogical discussions. Students played only their secondary instruments for this class. Were I to do this again, I would have these newly trained players on secondary instruments help teach the music education string classes for winds, brass, and percussion students. This could have been a heterogeneous class teaching experience needed to parallel the public school situation, and would have been beneficial for the wind, brass, and percussion music education majors.

It was rewarding to note a how qualified the music-ed string concentration students were becoming to handle instruction of string instruments. How much more competent these future teachers would be to evaluate their school's string groups having the knowledge to recognize faulty playing techniques and correct them. How much more comfortable they would be dealing with the problems of string performance than those who learned their craft in a homogeneous or heterogeneous class setting.

Education should be a setting that provides the most competent instruction, allowing reasonable time for learning in all areas directly related to the information and techniques a teacher will be charged with transmitting to others. It should require a course of learning that focuses primarily on the main subject areas of knowledge that they will be expected to teach. From what we are seeing in our public schools today, there must be other subject areas such as English, math, reading, and spelling that have not allowed enough time for teachers of these disciplines to study or focus. Not everyone who achieves a high level of learning through a meaningful education will be able to pass on information successfully. Teaching, as in performing, also requires an innate talent for communicating knowledge. On the other hand, if one does not have the in-depth education to acquire the knowledge one needs to communicate, one will merely become an inadequate instructor.

The issue of major importance is the available instruction necessary for string students in the music education program. Instruction by major faculty must be a specific requirement by Boards of Education for schools of higher education offering music education degrees in orchestral instruments. There will no doubt be numerous protests to this edict because it may impact college-level faculty who have no room on their schedules for more students. We must, however realize that providing instruction for music-ed students only by graduate assistants or associate instructors (who may only have just received their own undergraduate degrees), is inequitable. This dilemma must be resolved.

Orchestral Training

I have great admiration for what has been accomplished by double bassists and their teachers today, as compared to the era in which I was a student. Double bass sections today are equally competent to the other string sections of the orchestra. I have heard double bassists who have not made the finals at recent auditions who would have been welcomed by many fine orchestras fifty years ago. The level of playing and the number of qualified players have dramatically evolved over the last forty years.

Aside from the intense study of orchestral excerpts under the guidance of a teacher, it is essential to involve oneself in as much ensemble experience as possible. This does not mean sacrificing schoolwork or other important obligations; however, the more exposure and repertoire one can experience, the more qualified one becomes.

Having been raised in New York, opportunities for orchestral experience were endless. Upon graduation from high school, I managed to associate myself with a different orchestra every day of the week. This meant carrying a bass on the subways of New York, as having a car then was not an option. I learned more about repertoire and orchestra playing in that year than in any other similar period. Conductors of these groups ran the gamut from having a modest ability to being quite competent. Even if I didn't learn much from a conductor, I was still learning a good deal of orchestral literature and getting more and more competent in ensemble playing. Participating in many groups required learning to work with different stand partners, and at other times it meant being the only bassist in a group. The latter made me realize the need to blend with the other string instruments, especially the cello. This was an extremely meaningful and essential experience, making me aware of tonal qualities and what I needed produce.

Extra involvement in pre-professional ensemble playing can be an education that matures and accelerates one's playing prowess. Capping this type of experience is becoming part of a young professional training orchestra like the National Orchestral Association in New York or the Chicago Civic Orchestra. Similar orchestral organizations will also be found in other large cities. Not only do these organizations provide the benefit of performing with the more experienced young musicians but also make it possible to meet new colleagues, build musical relationships, develop new friendships, and may potentially result in making new contacts for professional involvements.

Learning and practicing orchestral repertoire alone in your studio is essential, but being able to use this knowledge in an orchestral ensemble is invaluable for learning style, intensity, and interpretation of orchestral works.

Music Schools and Education of Orchestral Musicians

Practically all music schools have orchestras, performance halls, orchestral rehearsal facilities, applied music teachers, practice facilities, conductors, and probably student conductors. Some may also have quality instruments to loan students.

Each one of the above has some impact on one's musical education. When choosing a school for the best educational opportunity, be aware that each of these aspects will affect the quality of your musical education.

First and foremost in importance is the applied music instructor. One needs more than an educational background to be a fine instructor. An instructor having an impressive orchestral background is most important. It tells you the instructor is a competent orchestral bassist, has experienced performing orchestral literature under competent conductors, and is more likely to have matured in his/her musical comprehension. A teacher who has had an impressive orchestral background in top orchestras need not have academic degrees to confirm his or her professional standing. Having academic credentials is fine but not a substitute for a meaningful orchestral performance background. Also determine if an instructor is qualified to teach the school of bowing (French or German) that you have studied. There are teachers who teach both schools of bowing and there are those who won't. If you have a way of knowing the success of a teacher's former students and their school of bowing, it makes it somewhat possible to judge how a teacher's qualifications may suit your needs. In addition to what you achieve in learning to make the best of your abilities, it is your major teacher who will be your main guide to succeeding professionally.

There are also very well qualified teachers who may not have had significant orchestral experience. You will be able to identify these people, as they are the very special double bass soloists of our time. They, too, have the special qualifications to be excellent instructors. They excel in the teaching of performance in the solo registers. Teachers on both ends of the spectrum can be of significant help in fulfilling the education of double bassists. It could be a definite advantage for a double bass student to be exposed to the teachings of both an orchestral bassist and a double bassist with a reputation in solo performance. If you are going to be an orchestral bassist, you should have experience with a teacher who can prepare you for this pursuit. A teacher's success can usually be measured by the success of his or her students.

The second most important faculty at a school is the conducting staff. It is their obligation to teach you how to listen for section and ensemble balance, be sensitive to musical phrasing, make proper articulations, and to perform repertoire that prepares you to audition for orchestral positions. Conductors who fulfill this prescription are not plentiful. It often takes higher salaries to attract fine professional conductors to academia than colleges and universities can afford. Conductors with high qualifications in the aforementioned areas are most often conducting one the country's top orchestras and not available for full-time academic positions. Some coaches in college sports may have an income equal to these very skilled professional conductors, but this level of income is sadly not available to conductors at university schools of music.

Fortunately, there are gifted and dedicated conductors who enjoy the challenge of training young musicians at top-level music schools. Their presence is also important in one's choice of a place to study. A good conductor will make much of your time in a school orchestra interesting, and challenging, and results in meaningful learning.

Other facilities important to the educational process include decent and sufficient practice rooms; large performance venues, recital halls, and safe instrumental storage.

The availability of competent counseling is very important. In many cases, your major instrumental teacher knows you better than anyone else and can be your best source for personal or academic counseling. If not, your teacher can point you in the right direction to find needed advice. Learn all you can about your potential double bass teacher. He or she will be your most important guide, advocate, and friend during college life.

Summers

CHOOSING AN EXPERIENCE BEST SUITED FOR PERSONAL ADVANCEMENT

There are numerous options for summer musical experiences. The best choice depends upon each student's musical and financial situation, and his or her personal preferences.

If one happens to be finishing the first year of college study with a new instructor, it might be wise to continue summer study with that teacher. Why? If the transition to college study has required making significant changes or adjustments in your playing habits, taking a break for the summer and going to another musical environment could result in some setback. If it is advisable to stay under the supervision of your principal teacher to keep moving in the right direction for the first summer, then don't be tempted to interrupt your personal progress.

For those who feel free to explore other universes musically, there are many summer programs. Various programs and workshops are geared specifically to the double bass, while others are strictly orchestral programs where no individual instruction or instrumental faculty is available. Some orchestral summer programs are very worthwhile, offering an opportunity to be exposed to a lot of new (and worthwhile) orchestral repertoire. A few are geared more to entertaining the public and don't offer that much to orchestra members in the way of a learning experience through performing meaningful orchestral literature. The latter situation should certainly not have any financial costs for the student and should provide a free ride, preferably in an attractive area of the country.

If you choose to attend a double bass workshop, make sure the "faculty" includes members or former members of top orchestras and/or respected solo performers. Remember that if you are primarily preparing for an orchestral career, orchestral performing ability is paramount even though a solo work is generally required at orchestra auditions. One needs to be a proficient performer in both aspects of playing. At times a student may tend to become overly enamored with solo playing and neglect proper dedication to orchestral excerpts. When one is caught in this dilemma, he or she needs to remember there are others studying who will be the competition, that are concentrating on becoming as proficient as possible in the orchestral repertoire.

Be very analytical about choosing a summer program. Ignore the attractiveness of brochures and study the content of each program. Know what you want from a program: orchestral experience; top-level double bass instruction; further study of solo literature; or perhaps just a summer spent in an appealing part of the country. Choose the latter only if you can afford the luxury of not needing more musical growth for a summer and know your playing will remain as competitive as necessary. Remember, there are always gifted and musical players working hard who will be your competitors for job opportunities. Developing to the best of one's ability in the study of orchestral instruments may mean choosing a situation for the summer that provides an opportunity for continued learning instrumentally and musically. That can mean going to the Aspen Summer Festival, Tanglewood, the Summer Festival at the Jacobs School of Music, or to other programs where there are fine teachers and fine orchestral programs.

Some Recommendations for Setting Up and Buying a Double Bass

Although I am not a luthier, many years of constantly asking questions of respected luthiers, doing some basic repairs myself, making a few bridges, experimenting with sound post placement, and even making the mistake of taking a double bass apart have provided me with some knowledge I believe allows me to give some basic advice. This is information a double bassist should have in order to make his or her instrument respond and play more comfortably. This is hopefully a guide to finding out what your instrument might require in order to be more user-friendly.

As you have probably already realized, double basses vary in shape, size, and playing qualities. In addition there may be the important physical adjustments that need to be made by a luthier. Usually there are adjustments that have to be made to make an instrument as comfortable to play as the instrument will allow. The personal playing habits of each player may demand an instrument be adjusted to accommodate them. This requires the double bassist to have some knowledge of what adjustments will be suited to his or her performance habits to achieve the optimum playing qualities of an instrument.

For example, I like to dig in when playing orchestral works. This means the bridge height would have to be high enough to allow this or the strings could rattle against the fingerboard. On the other hand, making the bridge higher also means more effort is needed by the left hand to depress the string. Finding the right string height can be a matter of compromise. Playing comfort for bowing and fingering has to be achieved. I use a minimum measurement of 4/16" between the string and top of the fingerboard (at the end of the fingerboard). Depending on the response of an instrument, I might use 1/32" more or less. Crucial to the proper adjustment here is the curvature of the fingerboard (lengthwise), which must be concave. This shaping must be done by a qualified repair person. It is not easy to achieve a perfect result, and this adjustment is not always done successfully. In addition to these adjustments, the depth of the grooves in the nut must also be properly adjusted so that there is a proper distance between the strings and the fingerboard adjoining the nut. (The proper distance between the bottom of these grooves and the fingerboard greatly affects left-hand comfort).

The next item that determines the level of comfort when playing is the bridge. The height is already determined by the distance of the strings above the fingerboard (as already described). There is also the distance between strings or notches across the bridge. This adjustment and the curvature of the bridge have to be considered together. In shaping the arch (top of the bridge), you will find that strings that are closer together will require a deeper arching than strings that are further apart, in order to obtain comfortable bow clearance between strings. The depth of the arch also controls how much pressure you can put on the bow before you end up playing on two strings rather than one. An arch that's too flat will result in less bow clearance. Too deep an arch will cause more effort and motion (bow winding) for string crossings. As you can see, all the factors affected by the physical measurement and shaping are very important in determining your comfort level for bowing and left-hand maneuvering. Some of these measurements might be made according to the usual practice used by the luthier. You might find these measurements very practical for yourself, or you may require some modifications that suit you better. Keep in mind the guidelines mentioned above to help you find the best set-up for your playing comfort.

Placement of the bridge should be centered on the f-hole notches laterally and vertically. A line made across the top from inner notch to inner notch should cut through the center of the side of each leg. The bridge should be placed evenly between the f-hole notches. Theoretically, this will produce the best tonal qualities and comfort, assuming the sound post is also properly placed. The sound post should be in line with the (G string) leg of the bridge, placed about the thickness of a sound post below the bridge leg. Further adjustments may be needed to find the optimum placing of the sound post for best tonal results. Rules of thumb: If the sound is too tight (resistant), move the post farther down (away) from the bridge. If the resistance of the string is too lax (spongy), move the sound post toward the bridge. Only adjustments of 1/16" in either direction should be made in each adjustment effort. A new evaluation will be required for each adjustment. Before moving the sound post, always loosen the strings enough to prevent the sound post from scarring the interiors of the top and back while it is being moved. Sound post adjustment can take time and patience. It should not be hastily done and should preferably be performed by a repair professional. Keep in mind that a sound post that's fitted too tight can crack or groove the top or back.

When loosening the strings to adjust the post, do not loosen them so much that either the bridge or post falls over. The instrument is more expanded in the summer, and a post can more easily fall during this warmer part of the year. When adjusting the post, it is visually tricky to make sure the post is standing straight. The f-hole provides a deceptive illusion of how straight a post is standing. You can look through the end pin opening in the bottom of the bass for a more accurate sighting for vertical positioning of the post.

It is generally believed that moving the post toward the G-string f-hole will increase the response of the upper strings and vice versa toward the E-string side. It is my experience that at times the result of moving the post toward the G string results in the G and A strings gaining more presence, and moving the post toward the E-string (minutely) affects the tonal qualities of the D and E strings. You will no doubt be determining this for yourselves when you go through the sound post adjustment process. The length of a sound post is also critical. Some players use two different posts, a longer one for warm weather and a shorter one for cold weather. A possible compromise is having a post cut and set during the in-between seasons when there are more moderate temperatures and humidity. Lastly, it is tricky to have the post fit just right. The top and bottom of a post must be angled a bit to fit the contours of the top and back. Use a sound post mirror to examine the fit of the post.

With all of this being said, there are construction aspects of a bass that can produce variables for aforementioned adjustments. For instance, if the angle of the fingerboard does not results in perfect centering of the board on the body of the bass, your bridge will have to be set to center on the fingerboard or the strings will not align with the fingerboard, making playing awkward. This will probably also affect the placement of the sound post to achieve the best tonal results. In addition, the location of the bass bar can also affect the proper placement of the sound post.

When we look at instruments critically, we find not only many variations in construction from one bass to another but also the formula used for measurements from one instrument to another can vary significantly. Some instruments may even have unequal dimensions for similar parts. I can only imagine that the availability of large enough pieces of wood may have at times been limited and forced a violinmaker to use what was available, even if it wasn't perfectly congruous. All of this means that one needs to be very critical when examining an instrument that is being considered for purchase. Sound, comfort, and condition should be prime considerations when appraising a double bass.

Going back to bridge construction, it is possible to choose between spacing strings closer together or farther apart. The closer together they are, the more curvature will be required of the playing arch of the bridge. The bridge shaping should be guided by personal preference. This can only be meaningful for someone who has experimented and who is very aware of the results of the various options of shaping.

Be aware that it is also possible to create more shaping compatibility between the bridge curve and fingerboard. It was pretty common that there would be distinct variance between the height of the G and E string at the end of the fingerboard. This also meant more left-hand effort to finger the E-string. Now we are able to get fingerboards that allow for more compatibility between the bridge curve and the arching of the fingerboard. Look for this when buying a bass or when having a fingerboard replaced. Basically, look for a more rounded fingerboard versus the board with a flat edge under the E-string. It will make a significant difference for left-hand and bow-arm comfort.

Awareness and Knowledge Necessary When Considering the Purchase of a Double Bass

Don't only buy an instrument because it was supposedly made by a famous old European maker. If the instrument doesn't have the sound qualities and playing response that should be present in a fine instrument, don't buy it hoping it will improve as you adjust to it. You wouldn't buy a car that wasn't comfortable and didn't perform positively for you, so why buy an instrument that doesn't complement you? When one auditions for a position, it is not the maker of the bass that the committee is interested in but rather the ability you display with an instrument that allows you to exhibit your competence most positively.

Be concerned with the physical health of an instrument. Note what repairs have been required and how well they were done. An unusual amount of repairs may indicate that the wood used in the bass tends to crack easily or may have had serious damage. An instrument that tends to crack naturally might be a constant source of costly repairs. Looking inside with a large sound-post mirror can be informative.

Look for depressions over the bass bar. If the bass has a flat back, note if it has been subject to many cracks. Flat backs can tend to crack more often as the wood dries.

Be concerned about the angle of the neck/fingerboard to the top of the bass. This angle can greatly affect the playing qualities of an instrument. The angle of the strings as they cross the bridge must not be too shallow, as this can cause too little resistance. A deeper angle creates more resistance. This angle can sometimes be changed to create proper resistance (tension) for your double bass; however, this requires some major changes, such as altering the neck angle and making a taller bridge. Don't buy an instrument with the thought that modification can make it sound and play as you hope it will. That is living on promises. Buy it only because you have tested it as recommended and because you are comfortable in that it complements your playing tonally and physically.

Make sure that the string length suits the size of your hand. A reasonable string length is between 41–42". Even if you have a large hand, realize that you will have more dexterity on a normal string length. Your facility need not be stretched to the max. You lose playing advantage by unnecessarily challenging yourself with long string lengths.

Necks should not feel too thick. This can hamper playing comfort and ability. There is even more to know when looking for a good instrument, but these are some basics. If possible, have an experienced professional examine and play the instruments you are considering. Compare the qualities of the instrument you are auditioning, with those of a fine double bass. Play and compare these instruments side by side in a concert hall. It is what an instrument projects that is so important, not only what one hears under the ear. An instrument may sound very satisfying when playing and standing next to it, but may be very disappointing at a distance. You want an instrument that projects your playing positively and audibly at a distance, as well as under the ear. The right-sounding bass can be very influential when performing at an audition or for an audience.

If any reasonable repairs and adjustments are necessary, that may be a secondary issue, as long as the basic qualities of the instrument are worth the investment. Perfect basses are extremely rare. I played only one in my lifetime and foolishly allowed the instrument to slip though my hands. A fine bass must have fine playing qualities, be comfortable to perform on, and must be in good physical condition. A footnote: on rare occasions basses can be found with worms. If they are still active, it is very costly and difficult to get rid of them. This is all the more reason for an experienced luthier to examine an instrument for invisible repair problems. Don't make a final judgment on buying a bass without seeking *unbiased* expert advice.

Information for Purchasing a Fine Bow

When hunting for a fine bow, test its balance by playing spiccato on all four strings. (The famous excerpt in Trio from Beethoven V is a perfect vehicle.) Allegros of some Mozart symphonies are also great for testing spiccato qualities. A fine bow will make these passages easier to articulate. A fine bow will make it comfortable to play an even-sounding, rhythmically accurate spiccato. For a bow's ability to sustain sound, try the thematic passage from Heldenleben and/or the Recitative of Beethoven's Ninth Symphony. Test playing forte attacks with the bow. Note if it helps in sustaining sound quality on the A and E strings. A desirable bow will help dig out the sound on the lower strings. Different bows may produce differences in the quality of sound when playing various articulations. Listen to a bow's tonal quality close up as well as at a distance by comparing it with the bow you are currently using or another fine bow with which you are familiar.

The quality of wood used for a bow is important in determining its playing qualities. The stick should be firm but not unusually thick. The weight should be a minimum of 135 grams for a French bow and about 140 grams for a German bow. These weights are not written in blood but are important guides to choosing a well-balanced bow. Keep in mind that density (stiffness, resistance) of the bow's wood is very important. The quality and quantity of sound a bow can produce are very dependent on the characteristics of the bow's wood. A soft wood will be spongy at the midpoint of the hair and usually will not produce impressive sonorities.

Normal lengths for the French model bow (stick only) are between 26 1/4–26 1/2". 26 inches is on the short side. Being this short serves no real purpose. This small difference from the normal lengths can be felt in sustained strokes. If, however, you find a really fine playing bow that is only 26", it would not be a mistake to purchase it, keeping in mind its shortcoming. I do not recommend buying a French bow any shorter in length than 26", as this will begin to affect the duration of a sustained bow stroke. You don't want to have to change bow direction, while the rest of the bass section is still sustaining the passage on one stroke..

Don't be impressed by unusually longer bows, as hair resistance tends to collapse more at mid-point on longer bows. A desirable bow will retain comfortable mid-hair resistance. The preferred length of the stick only on a German model bow is 27". All measurements of length refer to the stick of the bow, and do not include the bow screw.

Fine quality bows are usually made of Pernambuco wood. In recent years, snakewood has also proven to be a desirable wood for fine bows. The latter is a denser, heavier wood than Pernambuco and allows for bow sticks to be a bit smaller in diameter. Due to the density of snakewood, bows of this material can weigh the same as Pernambuco even when they are a bit smaller in diameter. Snakewood bows can be a little heavier than Pernambuco bows without being too heavy or clubby. A 145-gram limit is roughly reasonable for a snakewood bow.

The above guides for bow dimensions are very important but not inflexible. There may always be a fine-playing bow that is an exception to recommended dimensions. Do not start out by accepting an exception before you have thoroughly investigated the bow market and have the experience that justifies choosing the exception.

Don't test a bow by using it only to play all the solos you know without testing all of its playing qualities in passages similar to the orchestral works already mentioned. A bow that sounds good on the G and D strings but doesn't help with spiccato or drawing a full sound from the low strings is not a bow for all seasons. A really fine bow is not a friend you can be without. It works for you. It makes all playing more controlled and comfortable. It will aid in producing desirable tonal qualities. It is your medium for projecting your bass's qualities and your musical efforts.

PART 4

Analytical Phrasing and Bowing for Solo Works

Legato Phrasing: The Age of *Portamento* vs. the Slur

When *portamento* is used sparingly, it often adds interest and beauty to a musical phrase.

When most of the slurred/*legato* phrases are dominated by a constant use of *portamento*, then the simple beauty of flowing *legato* is gone. The phrase often suffers from a lack of continuity when overrun by the excessive use of *portamento*. I have unfortunately heard too many performances in recent years that suffer at the hands of the constant practice of the *portamento* and the absence of the beautiful uninterrupted flow of the legato indicated by the composer.

The *portamento* is too often being used as a gushing of musical expressiveness, but often ends up in a distortion and division of the composer's intent for a flowing phrase. We would not read every written line of poetry or prose, expressing each word this individually, so as to lose the overall message or thought the writer intended to express. Music is no different. It is sad when phrasing or consciousness of a phrase is intellectually not recognized, but it is also disturbing when a phrase becomes mangled by the exaggerated use of the *portamento*. As already mentioned, used sparingly and in good taste, *portamento* can be a welcome enhancement in phrasing, but using it as a constant interruption to the legato motion of a phrase is distortion. You only have to listen to the wonderful phrasing achieved by performers like Stern, Rostropovich, and Oistrakh to note that we have currently lost much of the beauty of legato phrasing to distortion through the overuse of the *portamento*.

Interpretation and Phrasing

Interpretation and phrasing are both difficult subjects to put into words or state definitively. There is so much inhibition about personal perception when phrasing; i.e., being solely influenced by what one's teacher advocated for phrasing in a particular work; blind adherence to the printed page; being totally devoted to one artist's interpretation above all others, and, most importantly, not really learning to make personal judgments about phrasing. It is impossible for a composer to transmit how he or she musically envisions the total interpretation of their music. There just aren't enough musical symbols available to make this possible. If there were, the process would require reams of additional space and a means of communicating every subtle nuance in the composer's mind. This leaves us with the most important obligation of creating phrasing that is based on an honest effort to interpret what we believe was in the composer's mind.

It is difficult to discuss phrasing if a mind-set has been created without due process of trying to glean the composer's musical intent. It is easier to discuss phrasing with students than with professionals, as students' minds are usually still open to criticism and discussion. Reaching the professional level can result in a mind-set that comes from consciously or subconsciously protecting one's intellectual turf. However, I will try and discuss phrasing objectively and (hopefully) impassionedly. Even in considering the factor of interpretation, there are aspects about phrasing that go beyond interpretation. When these are ignored, there could be some question about the validity of one's musical perception of a composition.

One of the most flagrant practices of string playing is the surging up-bow, most often not really inspired by phrasing or interpretation. In a 3/4 meter, if the first note is a half note, string players often increase the speed of the following quarter-note stroke without decreasing pressure on the bow. As a result we hear the disturbing anxious surge of the third beat in a 3/4 measure or similarly the fourth beat in a 4/4 measure. Oddly enough, the downbeat that follows is often some sort of resolution or culmination point in the phrase. Instead of the up-bow leading to the resolution or downbeat, its surging overshadows the importance of the resolution and puts the accent on the wrong "syllable."

Think of the beginning of the Star-Spangled Banner. The pick-up or third beat with the word "oh" should musically lead to the downbeat "say." The third-beat pick-up can enhance the downbeat "say" by leading to it, allowing for the downbeat "say" to be more prominent musically. However, "say" is still not the main focus in the phrase. It is also part of the phrase that is leading to the most prominent or important note in the first two bars. There is an ongoing increase in phrasing intensity leading to the first part of the (full) second bar, which culminates on the word "see." If the opening pick-up on the word "oh" overshadowed the downbeat "say," it would invalidate part of the total affect of a phrasing culmination on "see." Note below what phrasing should be attempted. All dynamics indicated are phrasing markings and not those generally used in notating the printed editions of the "Star-Spangled Banner."

The Star Spangled Banner

"A lot to do about not much," you may be thinking, but when you next sit in the audience or attend a concert, note how many surging up-bows there are that overshadow and distract from some more important down-bows (or downbeats), which are the desired points of resolution or musical focus for proper musical phrasing.

A universal example of thoughtless playing that creates negative phrasing is the unmusical approach to the opening measures of the Bottesini Concerto in B minor. There is the important sustained opening note, followed by five triplet eighths that should be leading to the downbeat of second measure. However, almost always, players surge on the first separate eighth note after the opening half note, making this eighth louder than any other note in passage. All of the eighth notes in the first measure should create a line leading to the downbeat of the second measure. Thus the five eighths start with softer, smaller bow strokes gradually getting louder while leading to the downbeat of the second measure, which should now be the fullest or richest sound since the opening (written A). There are many instances of proper phrasing being impacted by unaware negative usage of bow.

Prelude from Second Suite for Cello by J.S. Bach

Let us now examine the Prelude of the Second Suite for Cello by Bach. Each of the first three bars uses a similar figure, but each bar focuses on a second beat that is higher in pitch than the previous bar. The second beats should be lead to by the preceding eighth or sixteenth notes. Each bar gives the feeling of an overall rising line and rising intensity. Each second beat is very important and should be led to by the preceding eighth or sixteenth notes. The fourth bar begins to relax, especially through the slower motion provided by the three last eighth notes. Thus we have the first three bars, each leading to the second beat and each growing in intensity through the rising pitches of each bar culminating on the second beat of the third bar with the fourth bar relaxing the intensity of the first phrase and forming a bridge to the second phrase. In this next section, you will find two-measure sequences versus the one-measure sequences in the first three bars of the piece. In the second six bars you will find a declining character in the overall pitches, allowing intensity to relax from bar 5 and 6 through 9 and 10 with resolution in bridge bars 11 and 12, ending this eight-measure section. Somewhat typical of Bach and many other composers is using a sequence one or two measures long and building phrases by writing them on progressively rising or descending sequences. Much of the Prelude is made up of phrases containing one- or two-measure sequences and bridges. More importantly, you can quite easily plot your phrasing by following the line or direction, as we did in the first twelve bars of the Prelude. As stated, it is typical for music to have sequences that rise and fall, resulting in the building and relaxing of musical tensions.

We need to think about the printed page and how definitively the bowings and phrasing marks indicate the absolute intent of the composer. We have taken all kinds of freedoms with music of the baroque. Bowings are freely inserted by string players and slurs and other articulations are just as freely added by wind players. These are not necessarily right or wrong but are and have been an accepted practice for years. Analyzing music and identifying the phrases, periods, and sections, as well as determining the increase and decrease of musical tensions, will allow you to make decisions on appropriate bowings, articulations, and interpretive phrasing.

Analytical Phrasing and Bowing for Solo Works

Suite No. 2

PRAELUDIUM. Molto moderato (♩ = 69-72)

J.S. Bach

122

Analytical Phrasing and Bowing for Solo Works

Analytical Phrasing and Bowing for Solo Works

Dragonetti and Koussevitzky Concertos

When examining the Dragonetti Concerto in G major (A major), we note it is mostly without much in the way of bowings other than separate single strokes. By the time we have heard the first movement it is quite apparent how barren this work sounds. A great deal of it is due to the great lack of bowing (color) variety. If this were a work of the baroque era, which would not have been too many years before this concerto was written, no one would have played it with the preponderance of separate or single bow strokes (as was usually written). Slurs and combinations of slurs in addition to separate strokes would at least be minimally added by the performer. Think of all the varied bowing approaches that cellists use for the Bach Suites and all the editions of other important works for the violin and cello. This all seems to beg the question of what is the best treatment for works by composers like Dragonetti and even Koussevitzky. Their works have usually been considered so sacrosanct that we rarely dare to edit their music by inserting bowings, even some that might enhance the phrasing and musical intentions. Certainly the giants who wrote for violin, viola, and cello are equal to those who wrote for the double bass and multiple editions do exist for concertos for these instruments. Why isn't this privilege universal?

With this in mind, I am going to dare to take the liberty of making some bowing additions to the first movements of the concertos of Dragonetti and Koussevitzky. There will usually be a musical explanation for the editing.

Analytical Phrasing and Bowing for Solo Works

Concerto
for Bass

Dragonetti

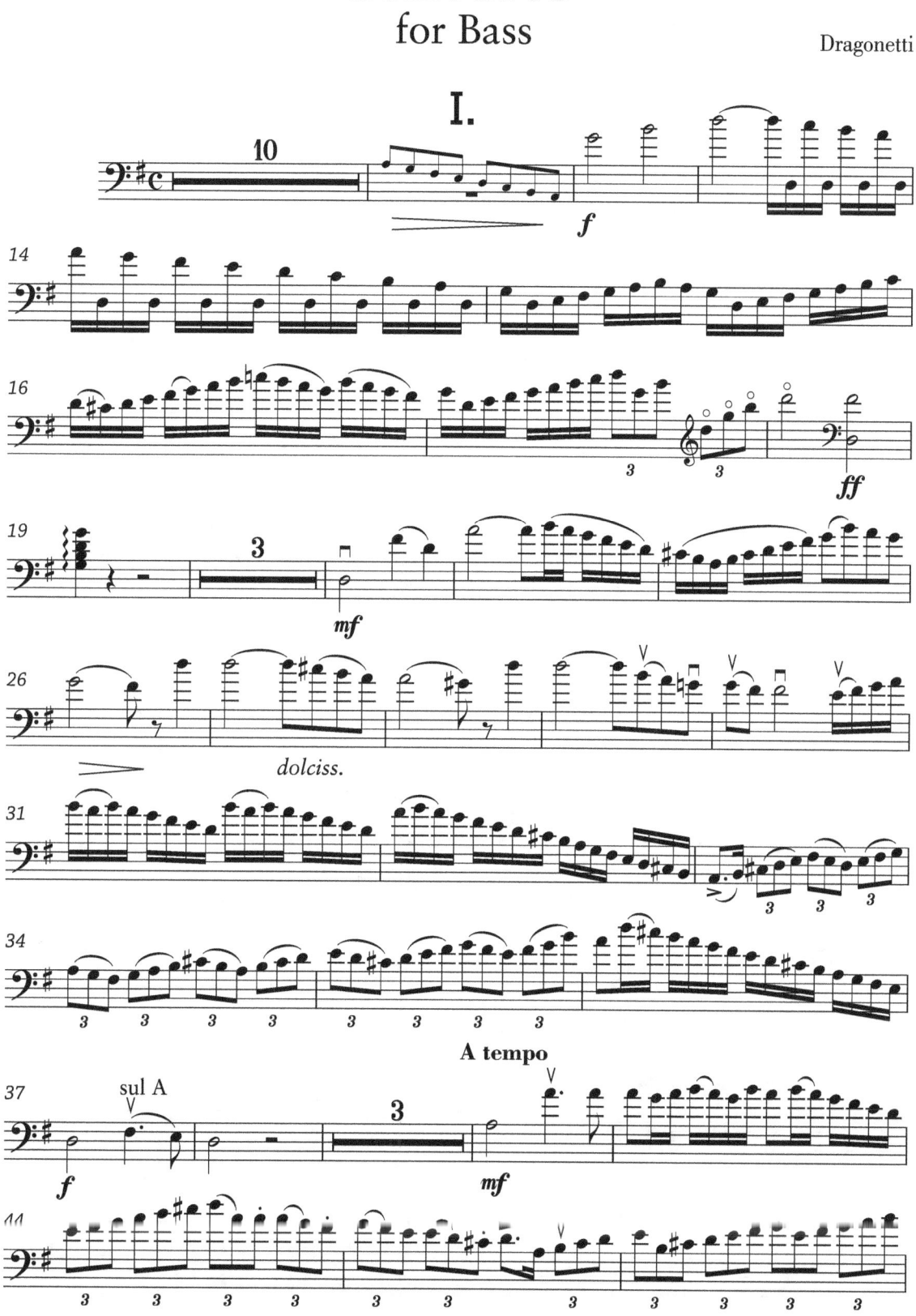

Analytical Phrasing and Bowing for Solo Works

126

Analytical Phrasing and Bowing for Solo Works

127

II.

Analytical Phrasing and Bowing for Solo Works

III.

Analytical Phrasing and Bowing for Solo Works

Analytical Phrasing and Bowing for Solo Works

Analytical Phrasing and Bowing for Solo Works

Phrasing and Bowing Suggestions for the Koussevitzky Concerto

On the following page you will find two short exercises designed to prepare for a more comfortable execution of the double stops in the first movement.

In the opening passage of the first movement of the concerto, the bowing has been changed in the second bar to allow a similar execution of the A# to C as presented by the first bar of the opening statement. These are presented as focal pitches by composer and the revised bowing of the second bar reinforces this opening fragment.

The same alteration is made in the second statement and is again a musical reinforcement of the interval of B to D used in opening of second statement.

You will note the bowing in the first phrase has been altered to allow the second phrase to have a symmetrical bowing pattern, since the second phrase is an imitation of the first phrase. The down-bow on the second beat of the third bar of this section should be played with a very soft legato and small amount of bow.

You will note parentheses around various dynamics. These are suggested phrasing dynamics and are to be used to contour a passage and not to create any exaggeration of phrasing or any dynamic alteration. You will note other markings with parentheses. They are all phrasing suggestions.

The phrasing of this first section, which ends four bars before the A tempo, should not reach its dynamic climax before the *ff* high E. Too often performers reach overly intense climaxes before this high E and thus diminish the intensity and focus of this more important climax.

In contrast to the quite melancholy opening of the preceding section, I would suggest the transition into C major encourages a more open and flowing sound. This initial presentation of C major should emulate the sun emerging from the clouds of the E minor section.

This section builds to the high F, which I have marked *ff* in contrast to the original marking of *forte*. The bowings also reinforce the intensity this section should achieve.

I have suggested an alternate bowing starting in bar 70 that I find provides a bit more needed intensity to the passage.

In bar 74, the suggested dynamic allows for building a more intense crescendo.

In bar 118, a separate up-bow is inserted to allow for more emphasis of a major climax in this movement.

In bar 129, the altered bowing allows for some contrast between the presentations of the similar figure starting in bar 137. It also allows for a more energetic climax for the second presentation of this figure, preceding the closing figure of the movement.

In bowing and marking dynamics in the second movement, I have again tried to enhance phrasing, stress climax points, and also provide comfort in bowing the technically more complex passages.

The recording by the composer clearly that establishes this movement was conceived to allow a great deal of freedom of interpretation. Subsequent recordings by other performers seem to confirm this observation. The bowings provided allow for this freedom of interpretation, as well as provide for performing movement with a more traditional approach.

The third movement mimics the first movement, as do the bowings suggested. I assume after the detailed explanation of bowing and phrasing for the first movement that the logic for added bowings and dynamics will be self-explanatory.

In the many years of teaching and experiencing performances of this concerto, the process of free-willed emoting and lack of awareness of results caused by careless bow usage constantly causes cringing at the unintended distortion of phrasing. Phrasing should be a result of your musical (emotional) reaction to a composition and your intellectual interpretation of what seem to be the composer's musical intentions.

Preparatory Exercises for Koussevitzky Concerto

These exercises are to prepare fingering for the double stops in the first movement of the Koussevitzky Concerto found in bars 129–132 and 137–140. They will help secure fingering and intonation.

Analytical Phrasing and Bowing for Solo Works

Editor's Note:
Dynamics in parentheses are added as phrasing suggestions by the editor to indicate increasing or decreasing intensities implied by the motion and direction of the musical lines.

Concerto
for Bass

Serge Koussevitzky, Op. 3

Excerpt from Concerto by Serge Koussevitzky
MGB Hal Leonard
Milan, ITALY

Analytical Phrasing and Bowing for Solo Works

Analytical Phrasing and Bowing for Solo Works

Analytical Phrasing and Bowing for Solo Works

II.

Analytical Phrasing and Bowing for Solo Works

139

Analytical Phrasing and Bowing for Solo Works

III.

Analytical Phrasing and Bowing for Solo Works

141

Analytical Phrasing and Bowing for Solo Works

142

PART 5

Preventative Exercises for Physical Abuses Related to Playing Double Bass

It's Usually Too Late When We Say "I Wish I Had!"

"You know, you have a bit of scoliosis," the therapist indicated. Why wasn't I surprised? I am a string player and spent a good deal of my life with one arm up to access the fingerboard and the other *down* maneuvering the bow. Just look around you when playing in an orchestra and study the various physical behaviors (playing positions) being employed. When you study these positions and become aware of the various physical postures being used, picture a person standing at ease. Note the difference compared to our performance posture as double bassists. One should begin to be aware of a string player's one-sided posture and understand why playing a string instrument results in physically abusive behavior. Over time, discomfort can result and possible injury to various body parts, including the spine.

We sustain unbalanced body behavior; practice for hours in one position, often going for long periods without even a short five-minute break. Signs of muscular strain and pain are ignored and we keep on playing. Generally we do not do any physical (re)balancing to offset the one-sided use we make of our bodies.

As double bassists, we have one arm up, the other down; both hands performing different chores. Heads are often tilted in one direction, in order to see the music stand or conductor. Legs are usually in an unsymmetrical position, while the torso is somewhat tilted forward. Is it any wonder that some of us complain about back fatigue and arm discomfort?

More abuse goes on, but enough has been brought to our attention to realize that performing on a musical instrument (especially of the string family) can result in physical damage, pain, and discomfort, even early in one's career. Generally, the presence of pain is when we begin seeking medical attention. That's when a physician may recommend physical therapy. At this point, it may take a long exposure to therapy to ease the discomfort. The pain may also tend to reoccur, and you may have to stop playing for a period of time in order to allow the inflammation to subside and heal.

There are ways that you may avoid this discomfort or minimize the damage required playing positions create.

1. Don't keep practicing when you feel strain. Don't wait for the pain. It takes only about five minutes of resting and massaging the tired arm muscles, which encourages circulation and relaxes muscular tension. About a half hour of intense practice might be followed by the resting/relaxing period just described. It is possible one can reach a need for this rest period even after 15–20 minutes, depending on the intensity of the physical demands of the music.
2. Think about our playing posture. We often tend to lift our left shoulders in excess, while performing. Try to avoid any excess of this habit, as it causes pulling on the back muscles and spine.
3. The left elbow in lower positions should not be elevated so that your arm is at right angles or more to the neck. You only need to achieve an elbow level that balances the usage of the left hand (fingers), allowing 1st and 4th fingers equal access to the string(s). Arm level should not cause a feeling of either of these fingers being tugged (pulled) away from the string. As previously stated, your position should result in the left arm and double bass neck creating less than a right angle (bottom side of arm to instrument's neck). The resulting position should not produce an unnecessarily elevated left shoulder (or a significantly drooping left arm).
4. Keep the right shoulder comfortably relaxed and relatively down or in normal physical attitude. The left arm/hand reaching into thumb position unfortunately will cause reaching out from the shoulder. Even in this position, do not pull shoulder out or up more than actually necessary.
5. Create a position of the bass that allows your bow arm access to the string without unnecessarily reaching around for the G string. Be careful of devices that require the right arm to be elevated due to the angle of the strings being raised, like might happen with bent end pins.
6. Don't reach out with the bow arm more than necessary, always retaining some bend in the elbow joint. Have your body travel with your bow arm enough to prevent unnecessary reaching out with the arm.
7. If you play sitting on a stool, always try and place your left foot on a low rung. Do not cramp the leg by an exaggerated bending at the knee, as a result of using too high a rung on the bass stool. Even with one foot on a (low) rung, try to balance the body (torso) as much as possible.
8. Do not lock the right knee in a straight position. Always maintain some bend in the knee, no matter how little.
9. Think of all motion as an integrated body movement. Do not isolate your efforts to single parts or joints. Feel energy and leverage flow from you as a

whole. Isolating the concentration of motion and effort (energy) to a single body unit will usually cause tension. This can also result in physical abuse that can irritate muscles and tendons.
10. Before problems arise from bodily abuse in playing, it might be helpful work with a therapist who deals with musicians and understands their required behavior. He or she can prescribe a short series of exercises that counteract exaggerated physical behavior required to play a string instrument. A simple example of balancing physical behavior would be for a left-handed pitcher or batter to perform right-handed. This rebalances the body usage and counteracts the strain and pain of performing one-sided. Interestingly enough, this reversing has been done with athletes. Although this seems illogical for the string instrumentalist, there are therapeutic exercises for us that can often help prevent the strain, pain, and malformation of shoulders, spine, etc. This therapeutic activity does not have to take a lot of time, *if* you use it as preventative for abuse rather than a cure for damage already done.

The following is written by Christopher Gales, a physical therapist for I.U. Health. I have had the good fortune to have a number of experiences with physical therapists and know how capable they are for treating our discomforts caused by abused muscles and tendons. Mr. Gales stands out as one of the extremely qualified and knowledgeable therapists I have encountered.

His following essay provides cause, effect, and suggestions for preventative behavior, basic information necessary for positive structural maintenance.

Playing Positions and Related Biomechanical Issues

Chris Gales

Chris Gales is a physical therapist at I.U. Health Rehabilitation and Sports Medicine Center in Bloomington, Indiana. He has a Doctor of Physical Therapy from Bellarmine University in Louisville, Kentucky. He also has undergraduate and masters degrees in Kinesiology from Indiana University, studying Clinical Exercise Physiology. Chris has worked in cardiac rehabilitation and physical therapy for twelve years.

(The information and statements in this chapter are not intended as professional or medical advice. Readers should consult with qualified Physical Therapists or medical professionals as to the appropriate exercises and other physical practices for their individual circumstances and condition.)

Professional athletes spend thousands of hours from childhood into adulthood practicing their sport. This is necessary to master the physical, fine motor, and cognitive demands of performing at a level of excellence attainable only by years of preparation. Athletes can sustain overuse injuries related to constantly performing the same set of movements on a daily basis.

Physical Therapies for Physical Abuses Related to Playing Double Bass

Professional musicians spend thousands of hours from childhood into adulthood practicing their instrument. This is necessary to master the physical, fine motor, and cognitive demands of performing their instrument at a level of excellence attainable only by years of preparation.

Musicians, like athletes, can sustain overuse injuries related to constantly performing the same set of movements on a daily basis to refine the skills needed to perform their instrument.

I understand that most bassists sit while playing their instrument, while others choose to stand to play. Some bassists may stand while practicing and sit when playing in the orchestral format. Mechanical concerns arise from spending long periods of time in either position. Whether seated or standing, bassists also tend to be tilted forward at the waist while playing, thus increasing strain on the back. The bottom half of the instrument being tilted forward causes the bassist to reach forward with the bow arm, increasing the reaching motion at the end of an up-bow. This further increases the load on the low back and arm.

When playing in the seated position, bassists often use stools with rungs. Most stools usually have 2–3 rungs at different heights, allowing the bassist to choose on which rung to rest the left foot in order to support the body of the bass. Some bassists do not use stool rungs, but instead opt to use a small platform like a classical guitar footrest.

Players who use the upper rungs of a stool hold their left hip and knee joints at more extreme flexion angles than those who use the lower rungs or a foot platform. The resulting increased hip and knee flexion angles when using the upper rung place a strain on both joints, as well as the muscles of the left leg. Over time, the accumulated increased stresses on the joints could contribute to cartilage breakdown, muscle imbalance, and increased muscle tendon or joint ligament laxity, leading to potential chronic pain and dysfunction.

One of Murray Grodner's former students has developed a chronically dislocating hip after years of sitting and positioning his left leg using stool rungs. Another bassist in the same bass section shares a similar problem. A dislocating hip is obviously a problem that could lead to surgeries as involved as an arthroscopic repair or even a total joint replacement. Although two bassists in the same orchestra with a similar ailment may be a coincidence, it is also likely the condition could stem from the chronic stresses they have placed on their hips over the many years and thousands of hours playing their basses while perched on stools.

Bassists who play in a seated position over a period of time need to be aware of the potential for the development of chronic injuries. They could address this issue by strengthening their legs (see "Mini-Squats," p. 152) and experimenting with different leg positions or platform heights to reduce the strain on the leg.

Stools designed specifically for bassists have a pop-out platform that sits about 4–6 inches off the floor. This design reduces the strain on the hip joint but still allows for the knee to flex at an angle sufficient to support the bass.

Those who stand to play generally place their left foot forward of their right foot.

Physical Therapies for Physical Abuses Related to Playing Double Bass

The stance is somewhat similar to a boxer leaning forward to jab. This foot position affords important leverage for playing the instrument in the standing position. Standing eliminates the problem of increased forces acting across the left hip and knee joints. However, standing and supporting the bass for hours of practice adds a new element of muscular endurance needed for the back and legs to hold a slightly flexed posture at the waist while playing. Engaging the core musculature (see p. 148–149) and keeping the back strong (see "Kick-Backs," p. 154) will help promote long-term comfort and function of the low back.

The Problem of Sharing Music Stands

In most orchestras, two players share one music stand. This requires each player's head to be turned toward the music stand that sits between them. The conductor standing at the front of the ensemble may be at a different angle from each player's perspective. Music stand partners sometimes wrangle about placing the music stand so that they can each have an optimal visual view of the conductor. This is more of a problem for the outside player than the inside player, because he or she is somewhat facing the back of stage when looking at the music. The result of chronically turning the head at an awkward angle to view the conductor and music could cause a stiff neck and sore muscles in the short term and could eventually lead to long term degenerative disc changes of the cervical spine. Of course the simple solution to this dilemma is a separate stand for each player, if one can convince management to incur the additional expense. A cheaper alternative may be to trade positions from time to time (see "Backward Shoulder Circles" and "Neck/Cervical Range of Motion," p. 151–152).

Posture

Keeping your back straight, chin up, shoulders back, and head held high is hard work, and can get downright tiring! It takes concentration and effort. Standing with good posture is especially beneficial. Sitting or standing with good posture takes muscle and tissue stresses off the joints. It can also help relieve the pain and discomfort associated with maintaining poor posture for long periods of time, causing overstretched muscles and tendons.

Ideal posture in standing involves standing up tall and positioning your head, shoulders, hips, knees, and ankles in a straight line. You can see what this feels like by standing with your back against a wall, making sure that your heels and the back of your head also are touching the wall.

Although no one is capable of maintaining perfect posture continuously, you can get much better at maintaining good posture with practice and persistence. Look in a mirror and stand up tall, with the best posture you can. Take a moment to think about how this position feels. Now start breathing again, because you may have been holding your breath while concentrating on how your posture feels. Try maintaining this good posture for as long as you can.

Most people have a hard time concentrating and holding good posture for longer than a minute or two. If you are one of the few who can effortlessly maintain perfect posture for hours on end, congratulations! Some people will slouch back into poor posture less than ten seconds after correcting, because as soon as they think about anything else, their posture returns to the position that requires the least muscular effort. The head and shoulders slide forward, and the thoracic spine, or mid-back, slouches into a flexed posture, held in position by the underlying tension/tautness present in the muscles. This tension can cause increased pain and soreness in nearby muscle groups, and then everything ends up hurting.

When you are playing seated for long periods of time, simply standing up from your stool and then sitting right back down will reset your posture and briefly relieve any tension stresses that were accumulating across your joints and muscles. In the practice room, try to stand up from your stool every ten minutes or so to reset your posture. Walk around briefly every thirty minutes when possible. Simply walking around the room or down the hall for a moment will do the trick. Although rehearsals can get long and breaks are limited, simply standing up from your stool for a moment between movements of a piece can be the brief chance you need to quickly reset your posture.

Although playing the bass requires you to hold specific postures, your body will still benefit from striving to work on maintaining good posture when you are not playing your instrument. Try to develop a personal reminder to reset your posture throughout the day. Whether sitting or standing, stand up tall and bring your shoulders back every time you check what time it is, walk past a mirror, see your reflection in glass, or every time you send or receive a phone call or text message. Developing a personal reminder to reset your posture will pay untold dividends over the course of your life.

Core Stability/Spine Mechanics

"Core muscles" refer to the muscles that surround your spine from both the front and the back. Thus, both your abdominal muscles as well as your lower back muscles contribute to your "core." The muscle groups in the stomach and the back work together to provide support to your spine, which comprises the vertebrae stacked vertically with the intervertebral discs lying between each vertebrae. Many muscles in your back and stomach are activated automatically, or involuntarily, when you move. Once you move a limb, muscles are activated that either help you move a body part or maintain a position or posture.

The core musculature is constantly involved when playing classical bass in either the seated or standing positions. When you lean forward to play up-bow and then lean back to pull the down-bow, your core musculature helps regulate the smooth movement of your trunk, torso, and upper body.

Although the core musculature acts involuntarily, you can consciously recruit the muscles in your stomach and back by tightening or drawing in your abdominal muscles. Think about tightening your abdominals as if someone was going to punch you in the stomach. Draw in your belly button toward your spine and hold it there for a few seconds. Another way to think about it is to tighten your pelvic or abdominal muscles like you would if you needed to go to the bathroom while driving, and the next rest stop on the interstate was twenty-five miles away. As you try this, lightly place your hands on the muscles of your low back on either side of your spine. As you tighten your stomach, you will feel the muscles in your low back tighten up as well. This co-contraction between the abdominal and low back muscles creates a drawstring or corset effect that provides support for the structures of the spine, like a built-in back brace.

Learning to voluntarily recruit your core musculature by sucking in your stomach muscles and holding them mildly tight (about fifty percent of maximum) while playing will cause your body to recruit more muscles to support your playing position. This will reduce strain on your back and potentially improve your endurance and comfort while playing for long periods of time.

Of course, trying to develop a new motor plan to recruit your abdominals and keep them tight while you are concentrating on the various cognitive and physical demands of playing may seem overwhelming. However, when not playing, you can start by practicing keeping your stomach muscles tight while maintaining a steady breathing pattern. Hold the fifty-percent maximum abdominal contractions steady for 5–10 seconds or so while still breathing, then relax your abdominals for a few seconds. Repeat 5–10 times.

Once you have gotten used to how it feels to keep your stomach tight and still breathe, progress to holding your abdominal muscles tight while walking. This adds another element of physical demand, causing your brain to focus on two or three different body movements at the same time. It represents a body coordination challenge similar to patting your head and rubbing your stomach at the same time. It may take some time to practice and master, so don't be discouraged if this is hard to do at first.

After mastering the task of walking while keeping your abdominals tight, try to incorporate keeping your abdominals tight while playing your instrument. Hopefully you will find that tightening your abdominals and keeping them activated while playing will reduce strain on your low back, providing a sense of a stronger, more stable core that may result in less back strain and soreness at the end of a long periods of playing.

Do not get discouraged if you find it difficult to incorporate this into your bass-playing body mechanics at first. Many individuals go through stages of being able to contract their abdominals and keep them tight while doing other tasks such as playing an instrument. You may start out feeling guilty for either forgetting to try or not being able to do it at all. Then you will begin patting yourself on the back for remembering to do it occasionally. Fully incorporating the new motor plan and regularly performing it subconsciously makes your back feel stronger and more stable in the long run.

If you give this abdominal recruitment strategy a try and either just can't get the hang of it or you feel no benefit from it, set the principle aside for now. If you ever experience low back pain and are referred to physical therapy, your PT will probably cover these principles with you and will be able to give you more training and feedback than this brief overview.

Arm Strength/Endurance

The group of muscles that drives the movement of your arm at the shoulder is collectively referred to as the "rotator cuff." Strengthening your rotator cuff muscles will improve the endurance of your left arm for maneuvering your instrument and fingering. It will also aid the right arm for maintaining the proper shoulder and elbow position while bowing. (see "Push-ups," "Resisted Rows," and "Resisted Arm Diagonals," pages 153–154.)

Scapular Mobility/Stability

Your scapula, or shoulder blade, articulates over the back of your rib cage on your upper back in the area of the thoracic spine. The thoracic spine is the middle third of your spine that has ribs connected to the vertebrae. The scapula is surrounded by musculature that branches off in various directions to connect your arm to your rib cage and your head to your neck. Some of your shoulder muscles begin on the front or the back of your scapula and attach to the top of your arm. Other muscles run from the back of your skull and neck down to the top of the scapula. As you raise your arm up, or move it in almost any direction, your scapula slides over the rib cage. The scapular muscles need to be loose and mobile to allow for ease of arm and neck movement, yet strong to promote good posture and allow for the efficient transfer of power from your arm through the bow to the bass. (See "Backward Shoulder Circles," p. 151; "Push-ups," "Resisted Rows," and "Resisted Arm Diagonals," pages 153–154).

Exercises to Reduce the Impact of Prolonged Postures and Repetitive Loading

It is always a good idea to check with your doctor before beginning a new exercise program to ensure that the new increase in activity level will not place you at risk for any unforeseen side effects related to your individual health history.

These exercises can be performed in a few minutes during practice breaks to help reduce the strain on your body related to the prolonged postures and limb positions associated with playing for hours on end. Perform each of the exercises to the right and the left, but do a few extra repetitions to the side opposite the position you are in when playing your instrument. This will help offset the wear and tear of the prolonged positioning. For example, since your torso is turned to the left toward the instrument when bowing, do a few extra trunk twists to the right. This will give your spine's joints and muscles on the right side a little extra work and help to balance out the demand on your back during the course of a practice session or rehearsal.

Do not be overwhelmed or intimidated by the length of the instructions you are about to read! These movements are fairly easy and intuitive. After you practice them a couple of times, you may not even need to refer to these instructions anymore. Figure out what works best for you. Some may decide to work through the whole list of exercises during rehearsal breaks, while others may try to steal a few repetitions of a specific exercise here and there over the course of a long rehearsal. There is no right answer for how often to do these exercises. Figure out what works best for you, and try to stick to it.

"Fast Four": Exercises for Preventive Maintenance in the Practice Room

1. Backward Shoulder Circles

Shrug your shoulders up, then pull them back, squeezing your shoulder blades together; then drop your shoulders down, completing the circle. Repeat 5–10 times.

Performing a few forward circles is also beneficial to include; but most of us tend to already have a forward shoulder posture. The backward circles are therefore more critical to help provide balance to posture.

2. Trunk/Low Back/Lumbar Range of Motion

Trunk flexion: Stand up straight with your feet about shoulder-width apart. Bend forward gently at the waist and drop your hands in front of you, like doing toe touches. Lean forward as far as is comfortable, but don't force anything. If you can only reach to your knees or just above them, don't be concerned! This should feel good, but not straining or painful. Hold the stretch for 2–3 seconds; then return to upright posture. Repeat 3–5 times.

Trunk extension: Remain standing upright with feet positioned shoulder width apart. Place your hands on your hips, and gently lean backward, feeling a stretch in your low back and tailbone area. You might feel a slight stretch on your abdomen as well. Hold for 2–3 seconds; then return to upright neutral posture. Repeat 3–5 times.

Trunk side bending: Stand upright in neutral trunk posture, legs shoulder-width apart, arms at sides. Slowly bend sideways (or laterally) to the right, dropping your fingers down the outside of your pant leg, until a gentle stretch is felt in your low back and side opposite the side you are leaning toward. (If you are leaning right, you will feel the stretch on the left side of your back and vice versa.) Start to one side, hold for 2–3 seconds, return to neutral posture, then lean to the other side for 2–3 seconds. Always come back to neutral in between side bends. Repeat 3–5 times to each side.

Trunk rotation: Stand upright in neutral trunk posture, legs shoulder-width apart, with arms relaxed at sides, and with elbows bent at ninety degrees. Now gently rotate your upper body to the right and left, holding to each side for 2–3 seconds and returning to neutral spine before turning to the other side. Repeat 3–5 times.

3. Neck/Cervical Range of Motion

The principles of performing this group of exercises are similar to the trunk range of motion exercises. These should be performed in a comfortable range of motion, never forcing anything into a painful end range. You may hear or feel occasional snaps, crackles, or pops in your neck or upper back when you do these exercises. This is nothing that should cause concern. The types of symptoms that should be reported to a doctor would include a repeatable, dramatic increase in neck pain every time you perform a specific movement (i.e. turning your head to the right) or any strange symptoms like sudden headache, dizziness, nausea, or numbness in your arm associated with a specific movement. This may indicate a problem with an intervertebral disc in your neck or a problem with blood flow through the vasculature in your head or neck.

Neck/Cervical Extension and Flexion: Slowly raise your head, looking up toward the ceiling until a gentle stretch is felt at the base of your skull, and hold for 2–3 seconds, then return to neutral posture. Then look down, with your chin toward your chest, and hold for 2–3 seconds before returning to neutral posture. Repeat 3–5 times up and down.

Neck Side Bending: Look straight ahead, then drop your ear toward one shoulder and hold the stretch for 2–3 seconds before returning to neutral. You will feel a stretch in the muscles of your neck on the opposite side. Then lean your head to the other side for 2–3 seconds. Repeat the brief stretch to the right and left for 3–5 times each. Remember, lean your head/ear toward your shoulder, but do not shrug or raise your shoulder toward your ear!

Neck Rotation: Turn your head to look over your shoulder to one side, holding a gentle stretch for 2–3 seconds. Again, you will feel the muscles stretch on the right side of the neck when you turn your head to the left. Hold each stretch to the right and left for 2–3 seconds, repeating 3–5 times to each side.

4. Mini-Squats/Deep Knee Bends

Weight lifters and athletes are not the only people who perform squats. You do it, too, every time you stand or sit. Squats use every major muscle group in the leg when performed, giving you a big bang for you buck for strengthening multiple muscle groups with one exercise.

Start out by standing and facing a counter, desk, or the back of a chair. Hold on to the raised surface with both hands, standing a couple of feet back so that your arms are somewhat out-stretched. Stand with your feet about shoulder-width apart. Now drop your bottom toward the ground in a squatting motion as if you were sitting in a chair. Bend your knees slightly as you drop your bottom, keeping your knees in line with your feet/ankles (don't let your knees knock together or sway out to the sides).

You should feel a slight strain or tension in your butt muscles (your gluteals) as well as the front and back of your thighs (your quadriceps and hamstrings muscles, respectively.) Start with a small mini-squat and progress to doing medium-range to deep squats.

A good way to make sure you are dropping your bottom toward the floor as you squat, and not just bending your knees under you, is to look down at your kneecaps as you perform the squat. As you squat down make sure that your kneecaps do not go past your toes. That is, you should still be able to see the tips of your toes over the front edge of your kneecaps at the bottom of your squatting motion while looking down at your thighs during the squat. After each squat, wait for a second or two. Repeat 5–10 times, and increase to doing 10–20 repetitions as the exercise gets easier over time.

For a slightly more challenging exercise, you can also lean back against a wall and slide down the wall, performing a wall squat. This helps ensure good form and a pure squatting motion through the exercise. Make sure to start with your feet out in front of you a little, while leaning back against the wall. Again, look at your kneecaps to make sure they do not overshadow your toes! Start out doing a mini-squat in this position, and increase the depth of the squat (as you get stronger), until you are literally sitting against the wall with your knees and hips at ninety-degree angles at the bottom of the squatting motion.

"Essential Four" Exercises to Strengthen Key Muscle Groups at Home

Time and space restrictions may limit what exercises you are able to do in a practice room. After all, you are there to *practice*, not work out! However, taking a few minutes at home to work through a few additional exercises will help you gain strength in key areas related to the prolonged postures and positions held throughout the body while playing the bass.

The first couple of exercises require no equipment at all and can be performed at the kitchen counter, a desk, or chair. The last couple are performed using resistive rubber tubing or Thera-Bands, which have been used in physical therapy clinics for many years. These products are now widely available at discount, department, or sporting goods stores in the exercise/fitness department. You could also shop online, using the key words "exercise tubing." Resistive tubing or bands come in various strengths, so start out with a light-to-medium gauge, and move up as you get stronger. Some models come with a strap in the middle that you can close in a bedroom or closet door to create an anchor point to pull from. Others can be wrapped around the other side of the doorknob of the room you are in and then secured by closing the door.

1. Wall or Countertop Push-ups: Chest, Arms, Shoulders, Core

Although push-ups and running laps around the gym or field have been used as punishment or discipline for years, they are actually extremely beneficial for physical fitness. Not only do push ups work the chest and biceps that we grow up associating them with, but they also work the scapular muscles that help you maneuver your instrument with your left arm and bow with the right. Push-ups also work your core musculature as you stabilize the rest of your body to keep your waist and hips from drooping down during the push-up motion. Tightening your stomach and focusing on staying stiff as a board during the exercise will help you recruit your core muscles, making your stomach and back stronger.

Push-ups do not have to be performed on the ground to be beneficial. You can do a push-up in a standing position by placing your hands about shoulder-width apart on a wall, counter top or desk top, leaning toward the surface, bending your elbows, and keeping your abdominals tight. Now push back out and straighten your elbows. Hold for a second or two and repeat. You can make the push-up easier by bending the elbows less, or make it harder by bending them more, thus bringing your chest closer to the surface you are pushing against. Start off doing 5–10 repetitions, and work your way up to 2–3 sets of 10–20 reps.

As you get stronger or want more of a challenge, you can certainly switch to doing push ups on the floor if desired. Don't feel obligated to do the latter, as you will still benefit from sticking to counter or wall push-ups.

2. Kick-backs: Low Back/Glutes

Stand at a counter, table, or chair and steady yourself with your hands on the surface. Keeping your legs straight, extend one leg slightly behind you until you feel a slight strain in the muscles of your low back. Don't overdo it! You do not want to strain your back while trying to make your hips, glutes, and back stronger! Start off doing this 5–10 times on each leg, and increase to 10–20 repetitions as you are able. You can either do separate sets of each leg, or alternate your kick-backs from leg to leg.

Also try tightening your stomach muscles, keeping them tight while you are doing the exercise. This helps recruit and use more abdominal and back muscles, helping to strengthen your core stabilizers.

3. Resisted Rows: Shoulder Blades/Upper Back

Secure the resistive tubing in a closed door or as directed by the tubing's manufacturer to create an anchor point, leaving two equal lengths of tubing to work with. Face the anchor point. Hold a length of tubing in each arm, stand up tall, then pull the tubing toward you and bend your elbows, like you are rowing a boat using oars. At the end of the rowing motion, squeeze your shoulder blades together to work the muscles between them. Repeat 10–20 times.

You can increase the resistance of the tubing by standing farther away from the anchor point, or make the resistance easier by standing closer to the anchor point as you are pulling the tubing.

4. Resisted Diagonals: Shoulders/Arms ("Bow Busters")

Face the door that is securing your tubing and grasp one length of tubing with your right hand. The other half of the tubing will be left dangling off the doorknob. Stand back far enough away from the door to allow light tautness or tension in the tubing. Try to hold your arm in the position it would be while starting a down-bow. Now pull the tubing diagonally away from the door as if you are pulling the bow. Pause briefly at the end of the motion, allowing moderate resistance. Start off doing 5–10 repetitions, and work your way up to 2–3 sets of 10–20 reps.

Now stand to the left of your anchor point, still holding the length of tubing in your right hand. Push your hand across your body, up and to your left, causing resistance similar to pushing your bow (up bow) across the strings. Start off doing 5–10 repetitions, and work your way up to 2–3 sets of 10–20 reps with mild to moderate resistance.

Although strengthening the same motions on your opposite side would not be critical to your bass playing, repeating each exercise with your left arm would promote muscle balance in your arms and chest.

Wrap-up

Performing each of these exercises at home 2–3 times per week will help you strengthen key muscle groups associated with dealing with the demands of playing the classical bass. They can certainly be performed daily if you find they are not taxing and are enjoyable, but 2–3 times per week will still get the job done.

Another critical component of overall physical fitness and health involves getting regular aerobic exercise, which is continuous exercise that raises your heart rate and keeps it elevated for a period of time. Examples would include activities such as walking, jogging, cycling, swimming, or using an elliptical machine.

A good way to judge the pace of the activity to gain aerobic benefit is to exercise at a late for a meeting pace, or the pace you would be walking across campus, across a parking lot, or down a hallway if you were late for a meeting or rehearsal! Another way to judge a mild-to-moderate pace would be to exercise hard enough that you are a little winded during the activity, but are able to maintain a broken conversation with someone else, pausing to take breaths occasionally, but not being so out of breath that you are unable to converse.

The American Heart Association recommends getting at least 150 minutes per week of moderate exercise. Another alternative is to get seventy-five minutes per week of vigorous exercise such as faster cycling, jogging, or playing pick-up basketball. Of course, you could also perform a combination of moderate and vigorous activity.

Exercising for thirty minutes a day, five days a week is a good way to divide the recommended weekly time requirement. However, you will still get health benefits if you divide the exercise time into two or three segments of 10–15 minutes per day. And if squeezing 150 minutes of exercise a week into your already busy schedule seems too daunting, remember that any increase in activity is beneficial for your overall health. So if you are not exercising at all right now, simply adding some aerobic exercise once or twice a week will be a great place to start.

As with any exercise program, discontinue any specific exercise if it is causing

Physical Therapies for Physical Abuses Related to Playing Double Bass

you pain beyond the normal mild muscle soreness associated with strength-training programs. This soreness should go away in a couple of days, and should eventually go away entirely if you get in the habit of performing these exercises regularly. If the pain persists, get examined by a qualified medical practitioner to ensure that no minor injuries become chronic problems that could potentially affect your ability to play and perform.

MURRAY GRODNER, Professor Emeritus, Jacobs School of Music at Indiana University, spent thirty-three years teaching double bass. His orchestral background includes playing Principal Bass of the Houston Symphony, Assistant Principal of the Pittsburgh Symphony under Fritz Reiner, NBC Symphony under Arturo Toscanini, Principal of the Sacramento Symphony, as well being a member of the San Diego Chamber and Louisville Orchestras. His chamber music background includes being a member of the Baroque Chamber Players and guest appearances with various chamber ensembles, including the Berkshire Quartet.

Publications include four editions of *Comprehensive Catalog of Music, Books, Recordings and Videos for the Double Bass*; *An Organized Method of String Playing, Double Bass volume*; co-author of *American String Teachers Associations String Syllabus* and numerous articles in *American String Teacher*; *The Double Bassist*, and *Bass World*.